MW00978054

MEN OF INTEGRITY

FACE TO FACE

An Encounter with Christ

The Lord would speak to Moses face to face,
as a man speaks with his friend.

Exodus 33:11a

PARTICIPANT'S GUIDE

FACE TO FACE
An Encounter with Christ

Published by

NelsonWord
MULTI MEDIA GROUP

A division of Thomas Nelson Publishers

Copyright © 2000 by Thomas Nelson Publishers

All rights reserved.

No part of this book may be reproduced, stored in a retrieval system, or transmitted in any form or by any means, electronic, mechanical, photocopying, recording, or otherwise, without the written permission of Thomas Nelson Publishers.

Unless otherwise noted, Scripture quotations are from The Holy Bible, New International Version. Copyright © 1973, 1978, 1984 International Bible Society. Used by permission of Zondervan Publishing House. Other Scripture quotations are from:

The New King James Version (NKJV), Copyright © 1982 by Thomas Nelson, Inc. All Rights Reserved.

The New English Bible (NEB), copyright ©the Delegates of the Oxford University press and the Syndics of the Cambridge University Press, 1961, 1970.

The Living Bible, (TLB) Copyright © 1971. Used by permission of Tyndale House Publishers, Inc., Wheaton, IL 60189.

The Message: New Testament with Psalms and Proverbs (The Message) by Eugene H. Peterson, Copyright © 1993, 1994, 1995, used by permission of NavPress Publishing Group. All rights reserved.

The New Testament in Modern English by J.B. Phillips (Phillips) published by The Macmillan Company, © 1958, 1960, 1972 by J.B. Phillips.

The New Century Version of the Bible (NCV), copyright © 1987, 1988, 1993, Word Publishing.

Printed in the United States of America
ISBN 0-8499-8826-8

For Information
Call Thomas Nelson Publishers 1-800-251-4000
www.thomasnelson.com

FACE TO FACE

An Encounter with Christ
Personal Commitment

Promise Keepers has designed FACE TO FACE men's retreat as a two-month commitment among the men of the church. We believe it is important to fully prepare our hearts and minds before we come into God's presence as a group of men seeking His heart.

Then, following the retreat, rather than return to "life as usual", it is vital for us to continue our daily disciplines. In this way, we will derive the greatest benefit from the work God began in our lives and in our church on our weekend away.

As a participant in this solemn assembly, you are asked to commit to the following:

> Daily read pre-retreat devotional material, journaling your thoughts and prayers for four weeks preceding the retreat;

> Daily prayer for at least the next two months;

> Daily worship, with appropriate worship CD or tape (best if immediately preceding or following devotions; e.g., can be done in the car on the way to work);

> Attend FACE TO FACE retreat weekend, participating in worship and small- group discussion;

> Daily read post-retreat devotional material and journal your thoughts and prayers for four weeks following the retreat;

> Continue to meet with your retreat discussion group once a week for four weeks following the retreat to complete the small-group Bible studies.

If you agree to above commitment, please sign and date this form, making a copy for your retreat leader as a confirmation of your planned attendance at FACE TO FACE: *An Encounter with Christ.*

SIGNED: _____ DATE: _____

WELCOME!

ELEMENTS OF YOUR GUIDEBOOK...

As you will note, there are four separate sections to this guidebook:

1. A four-week devotional for use before the retreat
2. An outline and discussion guide for the presentations at the retreat
3. A four-week devotional for use following the retreat
4. Four weekly Bible studies to complete with your retreat small group

Each of these is important, and each builds upon the preceding section(s).

SUGGESTIONS FOR EFFECTIVE USE...

This guidebook will be your companion for the next two months. It is your personal record of God's work in your life throughout this time of special commitment to Him and the men of your church. Please mark it with your name, keep it in a safe place, **and bring it with you to the retreat.**

As you will note, there are *six* devotions for every week preceding the event. Church attendance fulfills the seventh day on those weeks. There are only *five* devotions for each week following the retreat. In this case, one day is replaced by the group Bible study and Sunday is reserved for church.

For your devotions and prayer, find a place that is as quiet and free from distractions as possible. If you are a very early riser, you probably have no problem getting time alone at home. However, some men find it best to leave early for the office and complete their devotions before co-workers arrive and the workday begins. Others find time and space after the rest of the family goes to bed. Another good plan is taking your lunch to a quiet park and using your car for a prayer closet. Use whatever plan works best for you to find quality time with the Lord.

While you have committed yourself to faithfully pursue daily devotions, prayer, and worship, there may be times when it is not possible. If that happens, just go on to the next reading and make up the day you have lost, at some later date.

The questions following each devotional reading are only suggestions for thought. If the Lord is leading your thought in another direction, follow his lead by all means! Sometimes you will have very little to write in the blanks provided. At other times, you will overflow into the margins. The main thing is to write *some*thing every day. Keep in mind, this is your record to look back upon and marvel at God's faithfulness to you.

Most importantly, relax and enjoy the process. Remember, it is not what you do for God that ultimately matters, but what you allow him to do in and through you!

INTRODUCTION

In 1997, Promise Keepers gathered hundreds of thousands of men on the Mall in Washington, D.C. for a sacred assembly. These men went before God in repentance and prayer for their families, their church, their country, and their world. It was a profound and historic gathering. Perhaps you were there.

Many men from Calvary Church of Santa Ana went to the assembly on the Mall. As they returned home renewed and inspired, Sealy Yates, men's ministry leader at Calvary, thought this encounter with God should not end with just one day. He suggested they do a sacred assembly retreat for the men in their own church. They did—for two years—finding it to be a tremendous impetus for their men's ministry and the life of the church.

Sealy understood the importance of preparing their hearts for the retreat, just as they had for the Stand in the Gap assembly on the Mall. Each man who attended the retreat committed to reading a selected book and praying daily for a month preceding the event. Sealy wrote to his group leaders, "This Sacred Assembly is dedicated as a time to call upon Almighty God to accept our broken and humbled hearts. We want to pray for his blessing through us as the spiritual leaders in our homes, our church and our community."

Their comprehensive plan forms the basis for this Promise Keepers retreat kit. Promise Keepers is indebted to Sealy and the men of Calvary Church of Santa Ana for their diligence in seeking God to make the most of their time together and sharing the results with us.

CONTRIBUTING AUTHOR

MAX LUCADO
Minister of the Oak Hills Church in San Antonio, Texas; speaks daily on his national radio program, *UpWords*; author of numerous best-selling books, including *Just Like Jesus, In the Grip of Grace, When God Whispers Your Name, He Still Moves Stones, No Wonder They Call Him the Savior,* and *Six Hours One Friday.* **Selections from various books by Max Lucado form the meditations included in the devotional sections of this workbook.**

ABOUT THE SPEAKERS

TONY EVANS
Co-founder and Senior Pastor of Oak Cliff Bible Fellowship; founder and President of The Urban Alternative; serves as Chaplain of the Dallas Mavericks basketball team. B.A., Carver Bible College, Th.M., Th.D., Dallas Theological Seminary; author of *Let's Get to Know Each Other, No More Excuses*, and several other books.

JOSEPH STOWELL
President of Moody Bible Institute of Chicago since 1987; radio personality on Moody's *Proclaim!* and *Moody Presents* broadcasts; pastor for sixteen years prior to coming to Moody; author of fourteen books including *Far from Home, Shepherding the Church,* and *Following Christ.*

CRAWFORD LORITTS
Associate Director, U.S. Ministries, Campus Crusade for Christ; author of *A Passionate Commitment: Recapturing Your Sense of Purpose* and *Never Walk Away*; co-founder of Oak Cliff Bible Fellowship in Dallas, Texas; international conference and seminar speaker; 1997 co-chair of the National Congress on the Urban Family.

JACK HAYFORD
Senior Pastor, The Church on the Way, the First Foursquare Church of Van Nuys, California; key board member of several Christian organizations, including National Religious Broadcasters, Pentecostal/Charismatic Churches of North America, and Promise Keepers; author of more than two dozen books including *Worship His Majesty* and *The Key to Everything*; composer of nearly five hundred songs, hymns, and other musical works, including the widely sung chorus "Majesty."

Devotionals compiled and edited, and retreat discussion guides written by Mary Guenther, freelance writer and editor in Nashville, TN.

Nelson/Word Multi Media Executive Producer, Harry Clayton
Promise Keepers Project Managing Editor, Jeffrey A. Leever

TABLE OF CONTENTS

Page

PRE-RETREAT DEVOTIONAL   1

   WEEK ONE: *God's Love*   1

   WEEK TWO: *God's Grace*   15

   WEEK THREE: *God's Splendor*   29

   WEEK FOUR: *God's Call*   43

RETREAT DISCUSSION GUIDE   57

   SESSION ONE: *Men Raising the Standard*   57
   Tony Evans

   SESSION TWO: *Men of God's Word*   65
   Joseph Stowell

   SESSION THREE: *MEN WALKING WITH GOD*   73
   Crawford Loritts

   SESSION FOUR: *MEN OF WORSHIP AND PRAYER*   81
   Jack Hayford

POST-RETREAT DEVOTIONAL   89

   WEEK ONE:
   Dropping Your Rocks: Forgive and Accept   89

   WEEK TWO:
   Life on the Vine: Abide in Jesus   101

   WEEK THREE:
   An Inside Job: Renew Your Mind   113

   WEEK FOUR:
   Extending Your Arms: Love One Another   125

MEN'S SMALL GROUP BIBLE STUDIES   137

   WEEK ONE: *Power to Change*   141

   WEEK TWO: *Under the Circumstances*   142

   WEEK THREE: *Swimsuit Edition*   143

   WEEK FOUR: *Like a Good Neighbor*   144

FACE TO FACE
PRE-RETREAT DEVOTIONAL

*Week One
God's Love*

REMARKABLE

PSALM 103:1-5
Praise the LORD, O my soul; all my inmost being, praise his holy name.
Praise the LORD, O my soul, and forget not all his benefits—
who forgives all your sins and heals all your diseases,
who redeems your life from the pit and crowns you with love and compassion,
who satisfies your desires with good things so that your youth is renewed like the eagle's.

Something happened a few weeks ago that could be filed in the folder labeled "Remarkable." I was playing basketball at the church one Saturday morning. (A good number of guys show up each week to play.) Some are flat-bellies-guys in their twenties who can touch their toes when they stretch and touch the rim when they jump. The rest of us are fat-bellies-guys who are within eyesight of, if not over the top of, the hill. Touching our toes is no longer an option. Looking down and *seeing* our toes is the current challenge. We never touch the rim when we jump and seldom touch it when we shoot.

But the flat-bellies don't mind if the fat-bellies play. (They don't have a choice. We have the keys to the building.)

Anyway, a few Saturdays back we were in the middle of a game when I went up for a rebound. I must have been pretty slow because, just as I was going up for the ball, someone else was already coming down with it. And the only thing I got from the jump was a finger in the eye.

When I opened my eye, everything was blurry. I knew my contact lens was not where it used to be. I thought I felt it in the corner of my eye, so I waved out of the game and ran to the restroom. But after I looked in the mirror, I realized that it must have fallen out on the floor somewhere.

I ran back onto the court. The guys were at the opposite end, leaving the goal under which I had lost my contact lens vacant.

I hurried out, got down on my knees, and began to search. No luck. When the fellows started bringing the ball downcourt, they saw what I was doing and came to help. All ten of us were down on our knees, panting like puppies and sweating like Pony Express horses.

But no one could find the silly lens.

We were just about to give up when one fellow exclaimed, "There it is." I looked up. He was pointing at a player's shoulder. The same guy whose finger had explored my cornea.

There, on his shoulder, was my lens. It had fallen on him . . . stuck to his skin . . . stayed on his back all the way down the court while he jumped and bounced . . . and then ridden all the way back.

Remarkable.

Even more remarkable when you consider that the contact lens made this round trip on the back of a flat-belly. One of the guys who can touch the rim and his toes. Had it landed on the shoulder of one of the "top-of-the-hill guys," no one would have been impressed. Some of us have the mobility of grazing buffalo. But when you think of the ride the tiny piece of plastic took, when you think of the odds of its being found, you have only one place to put this event: in the folder labeled "Remarkable."

The more I thought about this event, the more remarkable it became.

The more remarkable it became, the more I learned about remarkable things.

I learned that remarkable things usually occur in unremarkable situations, i.e., Saturday morning basketball games.

Remarkable.

I also noticed that there are more remarkable things going on than those I usually see. In fact, as I began to look around, I found more and more things that I'd labeled "To be expected" that deserve to be labeled "Well what do you know."

Examples?

Each morning I climb into a truck that weighs half a ton and take it out on an interstate where I—and a thousand other drivers—turn our vehicles into sixty-mile-per-hour missiles. Although I've had a few scares and mishaps, I still whistle while I drive at a speed that would have caused my great-grandfather to pass out.

Remarkable.

Every day I have the honor of sitting down with a book that contains the words of the One who created me. Every day I have the opportunity to let him give me a thought or two on how to live.

If I don't do what he says, he doesn't burn the book or cancel my subscription. If I disagree with what he says, lightning doesn't split my swivel chair or an angel doesn't mark my name off the holy list. If I don't understand what he says, he doesn't call me a dummy.

In fact, he calls me "Son," and on a different page explains what I don't understand.

Remarkable.

At the end of the day when I walk through the house, I step into the bedrooms of three little girls. Their covers are usually kicked off, so I cover them up. Their hair usually hides their faces, so I brush it back. And one by one, I bend over and kiss the foreheads of the angels God has loaned me. Then I stand in the doorway and wonder why in the world he would entrust a stumbling, fumbling fellow like me with the task of loving and leading such treasures.

Remarkable.

Then I go and crawl into bed with a woman far wiser than I . . . a woman who deserves a man much better looking than I . . . but a woman who would argue that fact and tell me from the bottom of her heart that I'm the best thing to come down her pike.

After I think about the wife I have, and when I think that I get to be with her for a lifetime, I shake my head and thank the God of grace for grace and think, *Remarkable.*

In the morning, I'll do it all again. I'll drive down the same road. Go to the same office. Call on the same bank. Kiss the same girls. And crawl into bed with the same woman. But I'm learning not to take these everyday miracles for granted.

Just think, it all came out of a basketball game. Ever since I found that contact, I've seen things a lot clearer.

I'm discovering many things: traffic jams eventually clear up, sunsets are for free, Little League is a work of art, and most planes take off and arrive on time. I'm learning that most folks are good folks who are just as timid as I am about starting a conversation.

I'm meeting people who love their country and their God and their church and would die for any of the three.

I'm learning that if I look . . . if I open my eyes and observe . . . there are many reasons to take off my hat, look at the Source of it all, and just say thanks.[1]

BETWEEN YOU AND GOD

What are the things in your life that you have labeled "To be expected" that deserve to be labeled "Well what do you know"?

_____

_____

_____

What would you like to say to the Lord?

_____

_____

_____

_____

_____

_____

_____

---

[1] *In the Eye of the Storm*, pp. 67-70.

A DIFFERENT KIND OF HERO

PSALM 95:6-7
Come, let us bow down in worship, let us kneel before the LORD our Maker;
for he is our God and we are the people of his pasture, the flock under his care.

Behold a hero of the west: the cowboy.

He rears his horse to a stop on the rim of the canyon. He shifts his weight in his saddle, weary from the cattle trail. One finger pushes his hat up on his head. One jerk of the kerchief reveals a sun-leathered face.

A thousand head of cattle pass behind him. A thousand miles of trail lie before him. A thousand women would love to hold him. But none do. None will. He lives to drive cattle, and he drives cattle to live. He is honest in poker and quick with a gun. Hard riding. Slow talking. His best friend is his horse, and his strength is his grit.

He needs no one. He is a cowboy. The American hero.

Behold a hero in the Bible: the shepherd.

On the surface he appears similar to the cowboy. He, too, is rugged. He sleeps where the jackals howl and works where the wolves prowl. Never off duty. Always alert. Like the cowboy, he makes his roof the stars and the pasture his home.

But that is where the similarities end.

The shepherd loves his sheep. It's not that the cowboy doesn't appreciate the cow; it's just that he doesn't know the animal. He doesn't even want to. Have you ever seen a picture of a cowboy caressing a cow? Have you ever seen a shepherd caring for a sheep? Why the difference?

Simple. The cowboy leads the cow to slaughter. The shepherd leads the sheep to be shorn. The cowboy wants the meat of the cow. The shepherd wants the wool of the sheep. And so they treat the animals differently.

The cowboy drives the cattle. The shepherd leads the sheep.

A herd has a dozen cowboys. A flock has one shepherd.

The cowboy wrestles, brands, herds, and ropes. The shepherd leads, guides, feeds, and anoints.

The cowboy knows the name of the trail hands. The shepherd knows the name of the sheep.

The cowboy whoops and hollers at the cows. The shepherd calls each sheep by name.

Aren't we glad Christ didn't call himself the Good Cowboy? But some do perceive God that way. A hard-faced, square-jawed ranchhand from heaven who drives his church against its will to places it doesn't want to go.

But that's a wrong image. Jesus called himself the Good Shepherd. The Shepherd who knows his sheep by name and lays down his life for them. The Shepherd who protects, provides, and possesses his sheep. The Bible is replete with this picture of God. (See Ps. 3:2; Ps. 79:1-3; Ps. 80:1; Ps. 95:7; Ps. 100:3; Mt. 9:36; Lk. 12:32; Mt. 26:31; Heb. 13:20.)

We need a shepherd. We don't need a cowboy to herd us; we need a shepherd to care for us and to guide us.

And we have one. One who knows us by name.

I don't need to tell you why this is so important, do I? You know. Like me, you've probably been in a situation where someone forgot your name. Perhaps a situation where no one knew who you were—or even cared.

It's never easy to be in a place where no one knows your name, but few of us know this as much as John Doe No. 24. His story, as recorded by the Associated Press, reads like this:

> UNKNOWN SINCE '45,
> JOHN DOE TAKES HIS
> SECRET TO THE GRAVE
> JACKSONVILLE, ILL.
>
> The mystery of John Doe No. 24 outlived him. There were few clues when he was found, wandering the streets of Jacksonville in 1945, a deaf, blind teenager.
>
> Since he was unable to speak and his relatives could not be found, he was placed in an institution. He became John Doe No. 24 because he was the twenty-fourth unidentified man in the state's mental health system. Officials believe he was sixty-four when he died of a stroke at the Sharon Oaks nursing home in Peoria.
>
> John Doe's caretakers believe diabetes made him lose his sight, and records indicate he was severely retarded. But workers remember a proud man, more intelligent than the standard tests

showed. They remember the tantalizing hints to his identity–the way he would scrawl "Lewis" and his pantomimed wild accounts of foot-stomping jazz bars and circus parades. "It was so obvious from what he pantomimed that he had quite a life at one time," said Kim Cornwell, a caseworker. "Like my grandfather, he could probably tell funny stories. We just couldn't reach out enough to get them" . . . .

He had a straw hat he loved to wear and he took a backpack with his collection of rings, glasses and silverware with him everywhere. At Christmas parties he danced to vibrations from the music. Last Christmas the staff bought him a harmonica ....

At a brief graveside service last Wednesday in Jacksonville, a woman asked if anyone had any words to say. No one did.

Somewhere in the darkness of John Doe No. 24 there was a story. There was a name. There were memories of a mother who held him, a father who carried him. Behind those sightless eyes were eyes that could see the past, and all we can do is wonder, *What did they see? A kid with a cane pole on a muddy river? A wide-eyed youngster eating popcorn at a circus? A jazz band in New Orleans?*

No one will ever know. No one will know because he could never tell. He couldn't even speak his name. And on the day he died no one had words to say. What do you say when you bury a life no one knew?

It's easy to say this, but I wish I'd been there. I would have opened the Bible to the tenth chapter of the Gospel of John and read verse 3, "He calls his own sheep by name and leads them out" (NCV).

It's not true that no one knew this man's name. God did . . . and God does. And it's wrong to say that this man never heard his name. Who knows how many times God spoke it to him through the years? In the silence. Through the dark. When we thought he couldn't hear, who is to say he wasn't hearing the only voice that matters?

The Good Shepherd knows each sheep by name. He's not a cowboy, and we aren't cattle. He doesn't brand us, and we're not on the way to the market. He guides, feeds, and anoints. And Word has it that he won't quit until we reach the homeland.[1]

BETWEEN YOU AND GOD

When have you felt the sting of being faceless and nameless in an indifferent society?

_____

_____

_____

What would you like to say to the Lord?

_____

_____

_____

_____

_____

_____

---

[1] *A Gentle Thunder*, pp. 73-77.

A FATHER'S FATHER

MATTHEW 5:4
Blessed are those who mourn, for they will be comforted.

My child's feelings are hurt. I tell her she's special. My child is injured. I do whatever it takes to make her feel better. My child is afraid. I won't go to sleep until she is secure.

I'm not a hero. I'm not a superstar. I'm not unusual. I'm a parent. When a child hurts, a parent does what comes naturally. He helps.

And after I help, I don't charge a fee. I don't ask for a favor in return. When my child cries, I don't tell her to buck up, act tough, and keep a stiff upper lip. Nor do I consult a list and ask her why she is still scraping the same elbow or waking me up again.

I'm not brilliant, but you don't have to be to remember that a child is not an adult. You don't have to be a child psychologist to know that kids are "under construction." You don't have to have the wisdom of Solomon to realize that they didn't ask to be here in the first place and that spilled milk can be wiped up and broken plates can be replaced.

I'm not a prophet, nor the son of one, but something tells me that in the whole scheme of things the tender moments described above are infinitely more valuable than anything I do in front of a computer screen or congregation. Something tells me that the moments of comfort I give my child are a small price to pay for the joy of someday seeing my daughter do for her daughter what her dad did for her.

Moments of comfort from a parent. As a father, I can tell you they are the sweetest moments in my day. They come naturally. They come willingly. They come joyfully.

If all of that is true, if I know that one of the privileges of fatherhood is to comfort a child, then why am I so reluctant to let my heavenly Father comfort me?

Why do I think he wouldn't want to hear about my problems? ("They are puny compared to people starving in India.")

Why do I think he is too busy for me? ("He's got a whole universe to worry about.")

Why do I think he's tired of hearing the same old stuff?

Why do I think he groans when he sees me coming?

Why do I think he consults his list when I ask for forgiveness and asks, "Don't you think you're going to the well a few too many times on this one?"

Why do I think I have to speak a holy language around him that I don't speak with anyone else?

Why do I think he won't do in a heartbeat to the Father of Lies what I thought about doing to the fathers of those bullies on the bus?

Do I think he was just being poetic when he asked me if the birds of the air and the grass of the field have a worry? (No sir.) And if they don't, why do I think I will? (Duh . . .)

Why don't I let my Father do for me what I am more than willing to do for my own children?

I'm learning, though. Being a parent is better than a course on theology. Being a father is teaching me that when I am criticized, injured, or afraid, there is a Father who is ready to comfort me. There is a Father who will hold me until I'm better, help me until I can live with the hurt, and who won't go to sleep when I'm afraid of waking up and seeing the dark.

Ever.

And that's enough.[1]

---

[1] *The Applause of Heaven*, pp. 61-66.

BETWEEN YOU AND GOD

To whom or what do you turn when you need comfort? Is this effective?

_____

_____

_____

What would you like to say to the Lord?

_____

_____

_____

_____

_____

_____

_____

_____

_____

_____

_____

_____

_____

_____

_____

_____

WHAT WE REALLY WANT TO KNOW

ROMANS 8:35
Can anything separate us from the love Christ has for us? (NCV)

There it is. This is the question. Here is what we want to know. We want to know how long God's love will endure. Does God really love us forever? Not just on Easter Sunday when our shoes are shined and our hair is fixed. We want to know (deep within, don't we really want to know?), how does God feel about me when I'm a jerk? Not when I'm peppy and positive and ready to tackle world hunger. Not then. I know how he feels about me then. Even I like me then.

I want to know how he feels about me when I snap at anything that moves, when my thoughts are gutter-level, when my tongue is sharp enough to slice a rock. How does he feel about me then?

That's the question. That's the concern. Oh, you don't say it; you may not even know it. But I can see it on your faces. I can hear it in your words. Did I cross the line this week? Last Tuesday when I drank vodka until I couldn't walk . . . last Thursday when my business took me where I had no business being . . . last summer when I cursed the God who made me as I stood near the grave of the child he gave me?

Did I drift too far? Wait too long? Slip too much?

That's what we want to know.

Can anything separate us from the love Christ has for us?

God answered our question before we asked it. So we'd see his answer, he lit the sky with a star. So we'd hear it, he filled the night with a choir; and so we'd believe it, he did what no man had ever dreamed. He became flesh and dwelt among us.

He placed his hand on the shoulder of humanity and said, "You're something special."

Untethered by time, he sees us all. From the backwoods of Virginia to the business district of London; from the Vikings to the astronauts, from the cave-dwellers to the kings, from the hut-builders to the finger-pointers to the rock-stackers, he sees us. Vagabonds and ragamuffins all, he saw us before we were born.

And he loves what he sees. Flooded by emotion. Overcome by pride, the Starmaker turns to us, one by one, and says, "You are my child. I love you dearly. I'm aware that someday you'll turn from me and walk away. But I want you to know, I've already provided you a way back."

And to prove it, he did something extraordinary.

Stepping from the throne, he removed his robe of light and wrapped himself in skin: pigmented, human skin. The light of the universe entered a dark, wet womb. He who angels worship nestled himself in the placenta of a peasant, was birthed into the cold night, and then slept on cow's hay.

Mary didn't know whether to give him milk or give him praise, but she gave him both since he was, as near as she could figure, hungry and holy.

Joseph didn't know whether to call him junior or Father. But in the end he called him Jesus, since that's what the angel said and since he didn't have the faintest idea what to name a God he could cradle in his arms.

Neither Mary nor Joseph said it, but don't you think their heads tilted and their minds wondered, "What in the world are you doing, God?" Or, better phrased, "God, what are you doing in the world?"

"Can anything make me stop loving you?" God asks. "Watch me speak your language, sleep on your earth, and feel your hurts. Behold the maker of sight and sound as he sneezes, coughs, and blows his nose. You wonder if I understand how you feel? Look into the dancing eyes of the kid in Nazareth; that's God walking to school. Ponder the toddler at Mary's table; that's God spilling his milk.

"You wonder how long my love will last? Find your answer on a splintered cross, on a craggy hill. That's me you see up there, your maker, your God, nail-stabbed and bleeding. Covered in spit and sin-soaked. That's your sin I'm feeling. That's your death I'm dying. That's your resurrection I'm living. That's how much I love you."

"Can anything come between you and me?" asks the firstborn Son.

Hear the answer and stake your future on the triumphant words of Paul: "I am sure that neither death, nor life, nor angels, nor ruling spirits, nothing now, nothing in the future, no powers, nothing above us, nothing below us, nor anything else in the whole world will ever be able to separate us from the love of God that is in Christ Jesus our Lord" (Rom. 8:38-39 NCV).[1]

---

[1] *In the Grip of Grace*, pp. 179-180.

BETWEEN YOU AND GOD

Describe what you consider your most unlovable behavior. Ask God if he loves you even then?

_____

_____

_____

What would you like to say to the Lord?

_____

_____

_____

_____

_____

_____

_____

_____

_____

_____

_____

_____

_____

_____

_____

THE GOD WHO WON'T LET YOU FALL

JUDE 1:24-25
*To him who is able to keep you from falling and to present you before his glorious presence without fault and with great joy—
to the only God our Savior be glory, majesty, power and authority, through Jesus Christ our Lord, before all ages, now and
forevermore! Amen.*

I would like to confess a fall. I've kept it secret long enough. I can't deny the stumble; nor can I dismiss the truth.
I fell. There were witnesses to my slip. They can tell you. Graciously, they have told no one. Out of concern for
my reputation, they kept the event a secret. But it has been a secret long enough. The time has come for my
mistake to be shared.

I lost my footing at a family camp.

My daughters and I chose to climb a wall–a simulated rock climb. The wall is made of wood with occasional
rock-shaped fingerholds bolted into the surface. For safety, the climber wears a harness around his waist. The
harness is attached to a rope that runs up through a pulley and then down into the hands of a guide who
secures it as the climber climbs.

I gave it a go. What's a fifty-foot wall for a middle-aged author? I gave the guide the "thumbs-up" and began.
The first half of the trip I did well. About midway, however, I began to get tired. These hands and feet are not
accustomed to climbing.

With about twenty feet left to go, I honestly began to wonder if I would make it. I gave serious thought to telling
the guide just to pull me up the rest of the way. My fingers were sore, and my legs were starting to tremble, and I
was regretting every Big Mac I'd ever eaten, but the thought of surrender was lost in the cheers of my daughters
who were already on the top.

"Come on, Dad. You can make it!"

So I gave it all I had. But all I had was not enough. My feet slipped, my hands slipped, and down I fell. I fell hard.
But I didn't fall far. My guide had a firm hold on the rope. Because he was alert and because he was strong, my
tumble lasted only a couple of seconds. I bounced and swung in the harness, suspended in midair. Everyone
watching let out a sigh, and I gulped and resumed the climb.

Guess what I did when I made it to the top? Do you think I boasted? Do you think I bragged about conquering
the wall? No way. I looked down at the one who kept me from falling. "Thanks, pal," I told him. I didn't pat myself on
the back or raise my fist in triumph. I didn't ask everybody if they'd seen what I did. I did the only thing that was
right; I said thanks to the one who held me.

Would that all my tumbles were so simple. So brief. So harmless. They haven't been. I've been known to let go
of much more than imitation rocks. I've let go of promises and convictions. There have been times when my fingers
slipped off the very stones of truth I treasure. And I can't tell you how many times I've expected to hit the bottom
only to find myself suspended in midair, secured by a pair of nail-pierced hands.

"Try again," he urges. And so I resume.

You and I are on a great climb. The wall is high, and the stakes are higher. You took your first step the day you
confessed Christ as the Son of God. He gave you his harness–the Holy Spirit. In your hands he placed a rope–his
Word.

Your first steps were confident and strong, but with the journey came weariness, and with the height came fear.
You lost your footing. You lost your focus. You lost your grip, and you fell. For a moment, which seemed like
forever, you tumbled wildly. Out of control. Out of self-control. Disoriented. Dislodged. Falling.

But then the rope tightened, and the tumble ceased. You hung in the harness and found it to be strong. You
grasped the rope and found it to be true. You looked at your guide and found Jesus securing your soul. With a
sheepish confession, you smiled at him and he smiled at you, and the journey resumed.

Now you are wiser. You have learned to go slowly. You are careful. You are cautious, but you are also confident.
You trust the rope. You rely on the harness. And though you can't see your guide, you know him. You know he is
strong. You know he is able to keep you from falling.

And you know you are only a few more steps from the top. So whatever you do, don't quit. Though your falls are
great, his strength is greater. You will make it. You will see the summit. You will stand at the top and join with all the
others who have made the climb.[1]

---

[1] *A Gentle Thunder*, pp. 79-81.

BETWEEN YOU AND GOD

Have you ever stumbled in your quest to follow Jesus? Have you lost your hold on promises or convictions? Have you experienced the wonder of God's saving hand? Have you resumed the climb?

_____

_____

_____

What would you like to say to the Lord?

_____

_____

_____

_____

_____

_____

_____

_____

_____

_____

_____

_____

_____

THE GUEST OF THE MAESTRO

REVELATION 19:5
"Praise our God, all you his servants, you who fear him, both small and great!"

What happens when a dog interrupts a concert? To answer that, come with me to a spring night in Lawrence, Kansas.

Take your seat in Hoch Auditorium, and behold the Leipzig Gewandhaus Orchestra–the oldest continually operating orchestra in the world. The greatest composers and conductors in history have directed this orchestra. It was playing in the days of Beethoven (some of the musicians have been replaced).

You watch as stately dressed Europeans take their seats on the stage. You listen as professionals carefully tune their instruments. The percussionist puts her ear to the kettle drum. A violinist plucks the nylon string. A clarinet player tightens the reed. And you sit a bit straighter as the lights dim and the tuning stops. The music is about to begin.

The conductor, dressed in tails, strides onto the stage, springs onto the podium, and gestures for the orchestra to rise. You and two thousand others applaud. The musicians take their seats, the maestro takes his position, and the audience holds its breath.

There is a second of silence between lightning and thunder. And there is a second of silence between the raising of the baton and the explosion of the music. But when it falls the heavens open and you are delightfully drenched in the downpour of Beethoven's Third Symphony.

Such was the power of that spring night in Lawrence. Kansas. That hot, spring night in Lawrence, Kansas. I mention the temperature so you'll understand why the doors were open. It was hot. Hoch Auditorium, a historic building, was not air-conditioned. Combine bright stage lights with formal dress and furious music, and the result is a heated orchestra. Outside doors on each side of the stage were left open in case of a breeze.

Enter, stage right, the dog. A brown, generic, Kansas dog. Not a mean dog. Not a mad dog. Just a curious dog. He passes between the double basses and makes his way through the second violins and into the cellos. His tail wags in beat with the music. As the dog passes between the players, they look at him, look at each other, and continue with the next measure.

The dog took a liking to a certain cello. Perhaps it was the lateral passing of the bow. Maybe it was the eye-level view of the strings. Whatever it was, it caught the dog's attention and he stopped and watched. The cellist wasn't sure what to do. He'd never played before a canine audience . . . and music schools don't teach you what dog slobber might do to the lacquer of a sixteenth-century Quarneri cello. But the dog did nothing but watch for a moment and then move on.

Had he passed on through the orchestra, the music might have continued. Had he made his way across the stage into the motioning hands of the stagehand, the audience might have never noticed. But he didn't leave. He stayed. At home in the splendor. Roaming through the meadow of music.

He visited the woodwinds, turned his head at the trumpets, stepped between the flutists, and stopped by the side of the conductor. And Beethoven's Third Symphony came undone.

The musicians laughed. The audience laughed. The dog looked up at the conductor and panted. And the conductor lowered his baton.

The most historic orchestra in the world. One of the most moving pieces ever written. A night wrapped in glory, all brought to a stop by a wayward dog.

The chuckles ceased as the conductor turned. What fury might erupt? The audience grew quiet as the maestro faced them. What fuse had been lit? The polished, German director looked at the crowd, looked down at the dog, looked back at the people, raised his hands in a universal gesture, and... shrugged.

Everyone roared.

He stepped off the podium and scratched the dog behind the ears. The tail wagged again. The maestro spoke to the dog. He spoke in German, but the dog seemed to understand. The two visited for a few seconds before the maestro took his new friend by the collar and led him off the stage. You'd have thought the dog was Pavarotti the way the people applauded. The conductor returned, the music began, and Beethoven seemed none the worse for the whole experience.

Can you find you and me in this picture?

I can. Just call us Fido. And consider God the Maestro.

And envision the moment when we will walk onto his stage. We won't deserve it. We will not have earned it. We may even surprise the musicians with our presence.

The music will be like none we've ever heard. We'll stroll among the angels and listen as they sing. We'll gaze at heaven's lights and gasp as they sing. And we'll walk next to the Maestro, stand by his side, and worship as he leads.

This story reminds us of that moment. It challenges us to see the unseen and live for that event. It invites us to tune our ears to the song of the skies and long—long for the moment when we'll be at the Maestro's side.

He, too, will welcome. And he, too, will speak. But he will not lead us away. He will invite us to remain, forever his guests on his stage.[1]

BETWEEN YOU AND GOD

Does the stress of life on earth obscure your vision of the eternal? What could you do to re-adjust your focus?

_____

_____

_____

What would you like to say to the Lord?

_____

_____

_____

_____

_____

_____

_____

_____

_____

_____

_____

_____

_____

_____

---

[1] *When God Whispers Your Name*, pp. 159-163.

Notes – Week One

14

FACE TO FACE
PRE-RETREAT DEVOTIONAL

Week Two
God's Grace

LISTLESS CHRISTIANITY

LUKE 23:33-34
When they came to a place called the Skull, the soldiers crucified Jesus and the criminals—one on his right and the other on his left. Jesus said, "Father, forgive them, because they don't know what they are doing." (NCV)

What's on your list?

Most of us have one. We think we are "basically good." Decent, hardworking folk. Most of us have a list to prove it. Maybe yours doesn't include cigarettes or AIDS. But you have a list.

"I pay my bills."

"I love my spouse and kids."

"I attend church."

"I'm better than Hitler."

"I'm basically good."

Most of us have a list. There is a purpose for the list: to prove we are good. But there is a problem with the list: none of us is good enough. No one. Not you. Not me. Not anyone. "All have sinned and are not good enough for God's glory."

Boom. So much for lists. So much for being "basically good."

Then how do you go to heaven? If no one is good, if no list is sufficient, if no achievements are adequate, how can a person be saved?

No question is more crucial. To hear Jesus answer it, let's ponder the last encounter he had before his death. An encounter between Jesus and two criminals.

All three are being crucified.

Tragedy reveals a person's character. And the tragedy of this crucifixion reveals that these two thieves had none. They slander Jesus with their last breaths. Can you hear them? Voices–husky with pain—sneer at the Messiah.

Every muscle in their bodies screams for relief. Nails pulse fire through their arms. Legs contort and twist, seeking comfort. But there is no comfort on a cross.

Yet even the pain of the spike won't silence their spiteful tongues. These two will die as they lived, attacking the innocent. But in this case, the innocent doesn't retaliate.

The man they mocked was half-dead. The man they mocked was beaten. But the man they mocked was at peace. "Father, forgive them, because they don't know what they are doing" (Lk. 23:34 NCV).

After Jesus' prayer, one of the criminals began to shout insults at him: "Aren't you the Christ? Then save yourself and us" (v. 39 NCV).

The heart of this thief remains hard. The presence of Christ crucified means nothing to him. Jesus is worthy of ridicule, so the thief ridicules. He expects his chorus to be harmonized from the other cross. It isn't. Instead, it is challenged.

"You should fear God! You are getting the same punishment he is. We are punished justly, getting what we deserve for what we did. But this man has done nothing wrong" (vv. 40-41 NCV).

Unbelievable. The same mouth that cursed Christ now defends Christ. What has happened? What has he seen since he has been on the cross? Did he witness a miracle? Did he hear a lecture? Was he read a treatise on the trinity?

No, of course not. According to Luke, all he heard was a prayer, a prayer of grace. But that was enough. Something happens to a man who stands in the presence of God. And something happened to the thief.

Read again his words. "We are punished justly, getting what we deserve... But this man has done nothing wrong."

The core of the gospel in one sentence. The essence of eternity through the mouth of a crook:

I am wrong; Jesus is right.

I have failed; Jesus has not.

I deserve to die; Jesus deserves to live.

The thief knew precious little about Christ, but what he knew was precious indeed. He knew that an innocent man was dying an unjust death with no complaint on his lips. And if Jesus can do that, he just might be who he says he is.

So the thief asks for help: "Jesus, remember me when you come into your kingdom."

The heavy head of Christ lifts and turns, and the eyes of these two meet. What Jesus sees is a naked man. I don't mean in terms of clothes. I mean in terms of charades. He has no cover. No way to hide.

His title? Scum of the earth. His achievement? Death by crucifixion. His reputation? Criminal. His character? Depraved until the last moment. Until the final hour. Until the last encounter. Until now.

Tell me, what has this man done to warrant help? He has wasted his life. Who is he to beg for forgiveness? He publicly scoffed at Jesus. What right does he have to pray this prayer?

Do you really want to know? The same right you have to pray yours.

It's more than we deserve. But we are desperate. So we plead. As have so many others: The cripple at the pool. Mary at the wedding. Martha at the funeral. The demoniac at Geresene. Nicodemus at night. Peter on the sea. Jairus on the trail. Joseph at the stable. And every other human being who has dared to stand before the Son of God and admit his or her need.

We, like the thief, have one more prayer. And we, like the thief, pray.

And we, like the thief, hear the voice of grace. *Today you will be with me in my kingdom.*

And we, like the thief, are able to endure the pain knowing he'll soon take us home.[1]

BETWEEN YOU AND GOD

What personal tragedy caused you to blame God for your pain? Have you made yourself "naked" before him?

_____

_____

_____

What would you like to say to the Lord?

_____

_____

_____

_____

_____

_____

_____

_____

_____

_____

_____

_____

[1] *He Still Moves Stones*, pp. 183-186.

LEMONADE AND GRACE

MATTHEW 14:25-33
During the fourth watch of the night Jesus went out to them, walking on the lake. When the disciples saw him walking on the lake, they were terrified. "It's a ghost," they said, and cried out in fear. But Jesus immediately said to them: "Take courage! It is I. Don't be afraid."

"LEMONADE, 5¢"

Norman Rockwell would have loved the scene.

Two girls sit on the sidewalk in little chairs behind a little table. The six-year-old is the cashier. She monitors a plastic bowl of change. The four-year-old is the waitress. She handles the ice. Pours the drinks. Stacks and restacks the paper cups.

Behind them, seated on the grass, is Dad. He leans against an oak tree and smiles as he witnesses his daughters' inauguration into capitalism.

Business has been steady. The Saturday-afternoon stream of patrons has nearly emptied the pitcher. The bottom of the cashier's bowl is covered with thirty-five cents of change. With the exception of a few spills, the service has been exceptional. No complaints. Many compliments.

Part of the success, though, has been due to the marketing strategy.

Our street doesn't get much traffic, so we did a little advertising. As my daughters painted the sign, I called several families in the neighborhood and invited them to the grand opening of our lemonade stand. So all of our clients, thus far, had been partial.

I was proud of myself. I leaned back against the tree. Closed my eyes. Turned up the radio I had brought. And listened to the baseball game.

Then I heard an unfamiliar voice.

"I'll have a cup of lemonade, please."

I opened my eyes. It was a customer. A real customer. An unsolicited neighbor who had driven by, seen the sign, stopped, and ordered a drink.

Uh-oh, I thought. Our service was about to be tested.

Andrea, the four-year-old, grabbed a cup that had already been used.

"Get a clean cup," I whispered.

"Oh," she giggled, and got a clean cup.

She opened the ice bucket, looked in, and then looked back at me. "Daddy, we are out of ice."

The patron overheard her. "That's OK I'll take it warm."

She picked up the pitcher and poured. Syrupy sugar oozed out of the pitcher. "Daddy, there's just a little bit."

Our customer spoke again. "That's fine. I don't want much."

"I hope you like it sweet," I said under my breath.

She handed the cup to the man and he handed her a dollar. She gave it to Jenna.

Jenna turned to me. "Daddy, what do I do?" (We weren't used to such big bills.)

I stuck my hands in my pockets; they were empty.

"Uh, we don't have any . . ." I began.

"No problem," he said, smiling. "Just keep the change."

I smiled sheepishly. He thanked the girls. Told them they were doing a great job. Climbed back into his car. And drove off.

Quite a transaction, I thought. *We give him a warm, partially filled cup of lemonade syrup, and he gives us a compliment and a payment twenty times too much.*

I had set out to teach the girls about free enterprise. They ended up with a lesson on grace.

And so had I. For all the theologizing we preachers do about God's grace, the kind stranger modeled it better than the best of sermons state it. For this story is the story of each of us.

Each of us has seen our ice melt in the July sun of stress. Who hasn't attempted to serve the best, only to find that the best has already been served and that the pitcher needs to be refilled? And there's not a person alive who hasn't wondered what God does when what we promise and what we produce aren't even close to being the same.

Lemonade stands and living life would be high-risk endeavors were it not for the appearance of gentle strangers on our streets. But, thank God, they come.

And, thank God, He came.

For isn't God the stranger who became our friend after looking past the dregs and into our hearts?

And aren't we not much more than surprised children, amazed that what we receive is twenty times, yea, verily a million times, more than what we ask for?

The next time your calm becomes chaos, think of that. The next time you find yourself in a storm and can't see God on the horizon, reflect on the lemonade stand. And if your walking on the water becomes floundering in the deep like Peter's did, lift your eyes and look . . . .

A Gentle Stranger may be bringing grace to your street . . . to your life.[1]

BETWEEN YOU AND GOD

Do you have a hard time receiving more than you think you deserve? What area of your life currently needs an abundance of God's grace?

_____

_____

_____

What would you like to say to the Lord?

_____

_____

_____

_____

_____

_____

_____

_____

_____

_____

_____

_____

_____

_____

---

[1] *In the Eye of the Storm*, pp. 253-255.

BORN ONCE OR BORN TWICE?

1 Peter 1:23

For you have been born again, not of perishable seed, but of imperishable, through the living and enduring word of God.

Changing the clothes doesn't change the man. Outward discipline doesn't alter what is within. New habits don't make a new soul. That's not to say that outward change is not good. That is to say that outward change is not enough. If one would see the kingdom, he must be born again.

That phrase, *born again,* belongs to Jesus. He first used it when he was talking to Nicodemus. Nicodemus was a good man. A very good man. He was a Pharisee, a religious ruler, a member of the Sanhedrin, one of the decision makers in Jerusalem. No doubt he had been taught and had taught that if you change the outside, you change the inside. He revered the law. He wanted to do right.

But Jesus told him, "I tell you the truth, unless one is born again, he cannot be in God's kingdom" (Jn. 3:3 NCV). Nicodemus's response is sincere. He didn't ask "Why?" He asked "How?" Perhaps you are asking the same question. How is a person born again?

To get an idea, think back to your own birth. Put the VCR of your days in reverse, and pause at your first moments. Look at yourself. Brand-new. New hands. New eyes. New mouth. No pre-owned parts. All original material.

Now tell me, who gave you these parts? Who gave you eyes so you could see? Who gave you hands so you could work? Who gave you feet that you could walk? Did you make your own eyes? Your own hands? Your own feet?

No, you made nothing; God made everything. He was the one who made everything new the first time, and he is the one who makes everything new the second. The Creator creates again! "If anyone belongs to Christ, there is a new creation. The old things have gone; everything is made new!" (2 Cor 5:17 NCV).

Here is (dare I say it?) the greatest miracle of God. It is astounding when God heals the body. It is extraordinary when God hears the prayer. It is incredible when God provides the new job, the new car, the new child. But none of these compares to when God creates new life.

At our new birth God remakes our souls and gives us what we need, again. New eyes so we can see by faith. A new mind so we can have the mind of Christ. New strength so we won't grow tired. A new vision so we won't lose heart. A new voice for praise and new hands for service. And most of all, a new heart. A heart that has been cleansed by Christ.

And, oh, how we need it. We have soiled what he gave us the first time. We have used our eyes to see impurity, our hands to give pain, our feet to walk the wrong path, our minds to think evil thoughts. All of us need to be made new again.

The first birth was for earthly life; the second one is for eternal life. The first time we received a physical heart; the second time we receive a spiritual heart. The first birth enabled us to have life on earth. The second birth enables us to have life eternal.

But the analogy contains another truth. May I ask another question about your birth? How active were you in the process? (Don't look at me like that. Of course I'm being serious.) How active were you? Did you place your hands against the top of the womb and shove yourself out? Were you in radio communication with your mother, telling her when to push? Did the doctor ask you to measure the contractions and report on conditions inside the womb?

Hardly. You were passive. You were not born because of what you did. Someone else did all the work. Someone else felt all the pain. Your mom did the pushing and the struggling. Your birth was due to someone else's effort.

The same is true for our spiritual birth. It is through God's pain that we are born. It's not our struggle, but God's. It's not our blood shed, but his.

Sin began when Eve looked at the tree (see Gen. 3:6). Salvation comes when we look to Christ. Astonishing simplicity. Summarized in the great promise of John 3: 16: "God loved the world so much that he gave his one and only Son so that whoever believes in him may not be lost, but have eternal life" (NCV).

God, the Lover. God, the Giver. God, the Savior. And man, the believer. And for those who believe, he has promised a new birth.

But despite the simplicity, there are still those who don't believe. They don't trust the promise. They can't imagine how God would know their name, much less forgive their sins. It's almost too good to be true.

If only they would try. If only they would test it. But God is as polite as he is passionate. He never forces his way in. The choice is theirs.

And for those who do come, he has promised a new birth.

Does that mean the old nature will never rear its ugly head? Does that mean you will instantly be able to resist any temptation?

Go to the delivery room to answer that question. Look at the newborn baby. What can he do? Can he walk? Can he feed himself? Can he sing or read or speak? No, not yet. But someday he will.

It takes time to grow. But is the parent in the delivery room ashamed of the baby? Is the mom embarrassed that the infant can't spell . . . that the baby can't walk. . . that the newborn can't give a speech?

Of course not. The parents aren't ashamed; they are proud. They know that growth will come with time. So does God. God is often more patient with us than we are with ourselves (2 Pet. 3:9). We assume that if we fall, we aren't born again. If we stumble, then we aren't truly converted. If we have the old desires, then we must not be a new creation.

In many ways your new birth is like your first: In your new birth God provides what you need; someone else feels the pain, and someone else does the work. And just as parents are patient with their newborn, so God is patient with you. But there is one difference. The first time you had no choice about being born; this time you do. The power is God's. The effort is God's. The pain is God's. But the choice is yours.[1]

BETWEEN YOU AND GOD

What evidence of new birth do you see in your own life?

_____

_____

_____

What would you like to say to the Lord?

_____

_____

_____

_____

_____

_____

_____

_____

_____

_____

_____

---

[1] *A Gentle Thunder,* pp. 108-111.

ON SEEING GOD

JOHN 14:8
Philip said, "Lord, show us the Father and that will be enough for us."

One of my favorite childhood memories is greeting my father as he came home from work. My mother, who worked an evening shift at the hospital, would leave the house around three in the afternoon. Dad would arrive home at three-thirty. My brother and I were left alone for that half-hour with strict instructions not to leave the house until Dad arrived.

We would take our positions on the couch and watch cartoons, always keeping one ear alert to the driveway. Even the best "Daffy Duck" would be abandoned when we heard his car.

I can remember running out to meet Dad and getting swept up in his big (often sweaty) arms. As he carried me toward the house, he'd put his big-brimmed straw hat on my head, and for a moment I'd be a cowboy. We'd sit on the porch as he removed his oily work boots (never allowed in the house). As he took them off I'd pull them on, and for a moment I'd be a wrangler. Then we'd go indoors and open his lunch pail. Any leftover snacks, which he always seemed to have, were for my brother and me to split. It was great. Boots, hats, and snacks. What more could a five-year-old want?

But suppose, for a minute, that is all I got. Suppose my dad, rather than coming home, just sent some things home. Boots for me to play in. A hat for me to wear. Snacks for me to eat. Would that be enough? Maybe so, but not for long. Soon the gifts would lose their charm. Soon, if not immediately, I'd ask, "Where's Dad?" Even a five-year-old knows it's the person, not the presents, that makes a reunion special. It's not the frills; it's the father.

We want God more than we know. It's not that we are greedy. It's just that we are his and—Augustine was right—our hearts are restless until they rest in him. Only when we find him will we be satisfied.

Moses can tell you. He had as much of God as any man in the Bible. God spoke to him in a bush. God guided him with fire. God amazed Moses with the plagues. And when God grew angry with the Israelites and withdrew from them, he stayed close to Moses. He spoke to Moses "as a man speaks with his friend" (Exod. 33:11). Moses knew God like no other man.

But that wasn't enough. Moses yearned for more. Moses longed to see God. He even dared to ask, "Please show me your glory" (Exod. 33:18 NCV).

A hat and snack were not enough. A fiery pillar and morning manna were insufficient. Moses wanted to see God himself.

Don't we all?

Alas, therein lies the problem: "But you cannot see my face," God told Moses, "because no one can see me and live" (Exod. 33:20 NCV).

According to legend, the first American Indian to see the Grand Canyon tied himself to a tree in terror.

According to Scripture, any man privileged to have been given a peek at God has felt the same. Sheer terror.

Remember the words of Isaiah after his vision of God? "Oh, no! I will be destroyed. I am not pure, and I live among people who are not pure, but I have seen the King, the LORD All-Powerful" (Isa. 6:5).

Upon seeing God, Isaiah was terrified. Why such fear? Why did he tremble so? Because he was wax before the sun. A candle in a hurricane. A minnow at Niagara. God's glory was too great. His purity too sterling. His power too mighty.

The holiness of God illuminates the sinfulness of man.

That's what happened to Isaiah. When he saw God, he didn't sigh with admiration. He didn't applaud in appreciation. He drew back in horror, crying, "I am unclean and my people are unclean!"

The holiness of God highlights our sins.

Listen to the words of another prophet. "Look, Jesus is coming with the clouds, and everyone will see him, even those who stabbed him. And all peoples of the earth *will cry loudly* because of him. Yes, this will happen!" (Rev. 1:7, emphasis mine).

The holiness of God highlights the sin of man.

Then what do we do? If it is true that "Anyone whose life is not holy will never see the Lord" (Heb. 12:14), where do we turn? We can't turn off the light. We can't flip the switch. We can't return to the gray. By then it will be too late. So what can we do?

The answer is found in the story of Moses. What did Moses do in order to see God? Read slowly what God says. You may miss it.

"There is a place near me where you may stand on a rock. When my glory passes that place, I will put you in a large crack in the rock and cover you with my hand until I have passed by. Then I will take away my hand, and you will see my back. But my face must not be seen" (Exod. 33:21-23 (NCV).

Did you see what Moses was to do? Neither did I. Did you note who did the work? So did I.

God did! God is active. God gave Moses a place to stand. God placed Moses in the crevice. God covered Moses with his hand. God passed by. And God revealed himself. Please, underscore the point. God equipped Moses to catch a glimpse of God.

All Moses did was ask. But, oh, how he asked.

All we can do is ask. But, oh, we must ask.

For only in asking do we receive. And only in seeking do we find.

And (need I make the application?) God is the one who will equip us for our eternal moment in the Son. Hasn't he given us a rock, the Lord Jesus? Hasn't he given us a cleft, his grace? And hasn't he covered us with his hand, his pierced hand?

And isn't the Father on his way to get us?

Just as my dad came at the right hour, so God will come. And just as my father brought gifts and pleasures, so will yours. But, as splendid as are the gifts of heaven, it is not for those we wait.

We wait to see the Father. And that will be enough.[1]

BETWEEN YOU AND GOD

Have you ever found yourself longing more for the gifts than for the Person of God? If so, what might that suggest about your relationship with him?

_____

_____

_____

What would you like to say to the Lord?

_____

_____

_____

_____

_____

_____

_____

_____

_____

_____

_____

_____

---

[1]Adapted from *When God Whispers Your Name*, pp. 171-178.

"DON'T FORGET TO LOOK AFTER ME"

2 Corinthians 12:9

[The Lord] said to me, "My grace is sufficient for you, for my power is made perfect in weakness." Therefore I will boast all the more gladly about my weaknesses, so that Christ's power may rest on me.

"Good, I'm glad you're sitting by me. Sometimes I throw up."

Not exactly what you like to hear from the airline passenger in the next seat. Before I had time to store my bag in the overhead compartment, I knew his name, age, and itinerary. "I'm Billy Jack. I'm fourteen, and I'm going home to see my daddy." I started to tell him my name, but he spoke first.

"I need someone to look after me. I get confused a lot."

He told me about the special school he attended and the medication he took. "Can you remind me to take my pill in a few minutes?" Before we buckled up he stopped the airline attendant. "Don't forget about me," he told her. "I get confused."

Once we were airborne, Billy Jack ordered a soft drink and dipped his pretzels in it. He kept glancing at me as I drank and asked if he could drink what I didn't. He spilled some of his soda and apologized.

"No problem," I said, wiping it up.

Billy Jack showed me his cassette player and asked if I'd like to listen to one of his tapes. "I brought my favorites," he smiled, handing me the sound tracks from *The Little Mermaid, Aladdin,* and *The Lion King.*

When he started playing with his Nintendo Game Boy, I tried to doze off. That's when he started making noises with his mouth, imitating a trumpet. "I can sound like the ocean, too," he bragged, swishing spit back and forth in his cheeks. (Didn't sound like the ocean, but I didn't tell him.)

Billy Jack was a little boy in a big body. "Can clouds hit the ground?" he asked me. I started to answer, but he looked back out the window like he'd never asked. Unashamed of his needs, he didn't let a flight attendant pass without a reminder: "Don't forget to look after me."

When they brought the food: "Don't forget to look after me."

When they brought more drinks: "Don't forget to look after me."

When any attendant would pass, Billy Jack would urge: "Don't forget to look after me."

I honestly can't think of one time Billy Jack didn't remind the crew that he needed attention. The rest of us didn't. We never asked for help. We were grownups. Sophisticated. Self-reliant. Seasoned travelers. Most of us didn't even listen to the emergency landing instructions. (Billy Jack asked me to explain them to him.)

An epistle to challenge the self-sufficient, Romans was written for folks like us. Confession of need is admission of weakness, something we are slow to do. That's why I think Billy Jack would have understood grace. It occurred to me that he was the safest person on the flight. Had the plane encountered trouble, he would have received primary assistance. The flight attendants would have bypassed me and gone to him. Why? He had placed himself in the care of someone stronger.

Again I ask, have you?

One thing's for sure: You cannot save yourself. The river is too strong; the distance is too great. God has sent his firstborn Son to carry you home. Are you firmly in the grip of his grace? I pray that you are. I *earnestly* pray that you are.

Do you live in fear of never doing enough? Or do you live in gratitude, knowing enough has already been done?

Do you have a small circle, accepting only the few who work like you? Or do you have a large circle, accepting all who love who you love?

Do you worship to impress God? Or do you worship to thank God?

Do you do good deeds in order to be saved? Or do you do good deeds because you are saved?

Do you pray, "God, I thank you that I am not like other people who steal, cheat, or take part in adultery"?

Or do you confess, "God, have mercy on me, a sinner"?

One last thought. Billy Jack spent the final hour of the flight with his head on my shoulder, his hands folded between his knees. Just when I thought he was asleep, his head popped up and he said, "My dad is going to meet me at the airport. I can't wait to see him because he watches after me."

Paul would have liked Billy Jack.[1]

---

[1] *In the Grip of Grace*, pp. 181-184.

BETWEEN YOU AND GOD

When have you tried to be strong in your own power when it would have been better to be weak, trusting in the Lord's power?

_____

_____

_____

What would you like to say to the Lord?

_____

_____

_____

_____

_____

_____

_____

_____

_____

_____

_____

_____

_____

_____

GRACE WORKS

ROMANS 6:1-2
"So do you think we should continue sinning so that God will give us even more grace? No! How can we who died to sin still live in it?" (RSV)

The Apostle Paul asks a crucial question. How can we who have been made right not live righteous lives? How can we who have been loved not love? How can we who have been blessed not bless? How can we who have been given grace not live graciously?

He seems stunned that an alternative would even exist! How could grace result in anything but gracious living? "So do you think we should continue sinning so that God will give us even more grace? No!" (Rom. 6:1, RSV). The two-dollar term for this philosophy is antinomianism: *anti,* meaning "against" and *nomos* meaning "moral law." Promoters of the idea see grace as a reason to do bad rather than a reason to do good. Grace grants them a ticket for evil. The worse I act the better God seems.

What a scam. You mothers wouldn't tolerate it. Can you imagine your teenager saying, "Mom, I'll keep my room messy so the whole neighborhood can see what a good housekeeper you are"? A boss wouldn't let the employee say, "The reason I'm lazy is to give you an opportunity to display your forgiveness." No one respects the beggar who refuses to work, saying, "I'm just giving the government an opportunity to demonstrate benevolence."

We'd scoff at such hypocrisy. We wouldn't tolerate it, and we wouldn't do it.

Or would we? Let's answer that one slowly. Perhaps we don't sin so God can give grace, but do we ever sin *knowing* God will give grace? Do we ever compromise tonight, knowing we'll confess tomorrow?

Is that the intent of grace? Is God's goal to promote disobedience? Hardly (see Titus 2:11-12). God's grace has released us from selfishness. Why return?

Think of it this way. Sin put you in prison. Sin locked you behind the bars of guilt and shame and deception and fear. Sin did nothing but shackle you to the wall of misery. Then Jesus came and paid your bail. He served your time; he satisfied the penalty and set you free. Christ died, and when you cast your lot with him, your old self died too.

There is no need for you to remain in the cell. The thought of a person preferring jail over freedom doesn't compute. What does the prison have that you desire? Do you miss the guilt? Are you homesick for dishonesty? Do you have fond memories of being lied to and forgotten? Was life better when you were dejected and rejected? Do you have a longing to once again see a sinner in the mirror? It makes no sense to go back to prison.

Have we forgotten the mess we were in before we were united with him? I choose the word mess intentionally. May I share a mess I'm glad I am out of? My bachelor's apartment.

Of all the names I've been called, no one has ever accused me of being a neat freak. Some people have a high threshold of pain; I have a high threshold of sloppiness. Not that my mom didn't try. And not that she didn't succeed. As long as I was under her roof, I stacked my plate and picked up my shorts. But once I was free, I was free indeed.

Most of my life I've been a closet slob. I was slow to see the logic of neatness. Why make up a bed if you are going to sleep in it again tonight? Does it make sense to wash dishes after only one meal? Isn't it easier to leave your clothes on the floor at the foot of the bed so they'll be there when you get up and put them on? Is anything gained by putting the lid on the toothpaste tube tonight only to remove it again tomorrow?

I was as compulsive as anyone, only I was compulsive about being messy. Life was too short to match your socks; just buy longer pants!

Then I got married.

Denalyn was so patient. She said she didn't mind my habits . . . if I didn't mind sleeping outside. Since I did, I began to change.

I enrolled in a twelve-step program for slobs. ("My name is Max, I hate to vacuum.") A physical therapist helped me rediscover the muscles used for hanging shirts and placing toilet paper on the holder. My nose was reintroduced to the fragrance of Pine Sol. By the time Denalyn's parents came to visit, I was a new man. I could go three days without throwing a sock behind the couch.

But then came the moment of truth. Denalyn went out of town for a week. Initially I reverted to the old man. I figured I'd be a slob for six days and clean on the seventh. But something strange happened, a curious discomfort. I couldn't relax with dirty dishes in the sink. When I saw an empty potato-chip sack on the floor I—hang on to your hat–bent over and picked it up! I actually put my bath towel back on the rack. What had happened to me?

Simple. I'd been exposed to a higher standard.

Isn't that what has happened with us? Isn't that the heart of Paul's argument? How could we who have been freed from sin return to it? Before Christ our lives were out of control, sloppy, and indulgent. We didn't even know we were slobs until we met him.

Then he moved in. Things began to change. What we threw around we began putting away. What we neglected we cleaned up. What had been clutter became order. Oh, there were and still are occasional lapses of thought and deed, but by and large he got our house in order.

Suddenly we find ourselves wanting to do good. Go back to the old mess? Are you kidding? "In the past you were slaves to sin–sin controlled you. But thank God, you fully obeyed the things that you were taught. You were made free from sin, and now you are slaves to goodness" (Rom. 6:17-18).

Can a discharged prisoner return to confinement? Yes. But let him remember the gray walls and the long nights. Can a newlywed forget his vows? Yes. But let him remember his holy vow and his beautiful bride. Can a converted slob once again be messy? Yes. But let him consider the difference between the filth of yesterday and the purity of today.

Can one who has been given a free gift not share that gift with others? I suppose. But let him remember that he received a free gift. Let him remember that all of life is a gift of grace. And let him remember that the call of grace is to live a gracious life.

For that is how grace works.[1]

BETWEEN YOU AND GOD

Have you returned to the prison of sin in any area of your life? If so, what specifically?

_____
_____
_____

What would you like to say to the Lord?

_____
_____
_____
_____
_____
_____
_____
_____
_____
_____
_____
_____
_____
_____

[1] Adapted from *In the Grip of Grace,* pp 11-117.

Notes – Week Two

FACE TO FACE
PRE-RETREAT DEVOTIONAL

Week Three
God's Splendor

THEY'D DO IT AGAIN

Matthew 14:25-33
During the fourth watch of the night Jesus went out to them, walking on the lake. When the disciples saw him walking on the lake, they were terrified. "It's a ghost," they said, and cried out in fear. But Jesus immediately said to them: "Take courage! It is I. Don't be afraid."
"Lord, if it's you," Peter replied, "tell me to come to you on the water."
"Come," he said.
Then Peter got down out of the boat, walked on the water and came toward Jesus. But when he saw the wind, he was afraid and, beginning to sink, cried out, "Lord, save me!"
Immediately Jesus reached out his hand and caught him. "You of little faith," he said, "why did you doubt?"
And when they climbed into the boat, the wind died down. Then those who were in the boat worshiped him, saying, "Truly you are the Son of God."

They'd do it again. I'm confident they would. The disciples would get into the same boat and ride through the same storm. They'd do it again in a heartbeat. Why?
Because through the storm they saw the Savior.

Read this verse: "Then those who were in the boat worshiped him, saying, `Truly you are the Son of God.'" After the storm, they worshiped him. They had never, as a group, done that before. Never. Check it out. Open your Bible. Search for a time when the disciples corporately praised him.

You won't find it.

You won't find them worshiping when he heals the leper. Forgives the adulteress. Preaches to the masses. They were willing to follow. Willing to leave family. Willing to cast out demons. Willing to be in the army.

But only after the incident on the sea did they worship him. Why?

Simple. This time, they were the ones who were saved. This time, their necks were removed from the noose. Their bodies were plucked from the deep. One minute, they were dangling over the edge of the abyss, staring into the throat of the slack jawed canyon. The next, they were bottom-plopped and wide-eyed on the deck of a still boat on a placid sea.

So they worshiped. They did the only thing that they could do when their death sentence was stayed at the eleventh hour: They looked to the Eternal Governor who gave the pardon and thanked him.

When you recognize God as Creator, you will admire him. When you recognize his wisdom, you will learn from him. When you discover his strength, you will rely on him. But only when he saves you will you worship him.

It's a "before and after" scenario. Before your rescue, you could easily keep God at a distance. Comfortably dismissed. Neatly shelved. Sure he was important, but so was your career. Your status. Your salary. He was high on your priority list, but he shared the spot with others.

Then came the storm . . . the rage . . . the fight . . . the ripped moorings . . . the starless night. Despair fell like a fog; your bearings were gone. In your heart, you knew there was no exit.

Turn to your career for help? Only if you want to hide from the storm . . . not escape it. Lean on your status for strength? A storm isn't impressed with your title. Rely on your salary for rescue? Many try . . . many fail.

Suddenly you are left with one option: God.

And when you ask . . . genuinely ask . . . he will come.

And from that moment on, he is not just a deity to admire, a teacher to observe, or a master to obey. He is the Savior. The Savior to be worshiped.

That's why I'm convinced that the disciples would do it again. They'd endure the storm another night . . . a thousand other nights . . . if that's what it took.

A season of suffering is a small price to pay for a clear view of God.[1]

---

[1] *In the Eye of the Storm*, pp.185-187.

30

BETWEEN YOU AND GOD

When we experience suffering or pain as a Christian, we often forget how awesome God is and how difficult life can be *without* him. ***If someone were to ask you if you would give your life to God again today, what would you answer? What if your decision involved suffering to know him better?***

_____

_____

_____

What would you like to say to the Lord?

_____

_____

_____

_____

_____

_____

_____

_____

_____

_____

_____

_____

_____

_____

THE APPLAUSE OF HEAVEN

REVELATION 21:1-5A
Then I saw a new heaven and a new earth, for the first heaven and the first earth had passed away, and there was no longer any sea. I saw the Holy City, the new Jerusalem, coming down out of heaven from God, prepared as a bride beautifully dressed for her husband. And I heard a loud voice from the throne saying, "Now the dwelling of God is with men, and he will live with them. They will be his people, and God himself will be with them and be their God. He will wipe every tear from their eyes. There will be no more death or mourning or crying or pain, for the old order of things has passed away." He who was seated on the throne said, "I am making everything new!"

I'm almost home. After five days, four hotel beds, eleven restaurants, and twenty-two cups of coffee, I'm almost home. After eight airplane seats, five airports, two delays, one book, and five hundred thirteen packages of peanuts, I'm almost home.

Home. It was my first thought when I awoke this morning. It was my first thought when I stepped down from the last podium. It was my first thought when I said good-bye to my last host at the last airport.

Home. The longest part of going home is the last part–the plane's taxiing to the terminal from the runway. I'm the fellow the flight attendant always has to tell to sit down. I'm the guy with one hand on my briefcase and the other on my seat belt. I have learned that there is a critical split second in which I can bolt down the aisle into the first-class section before the tributaries of people begin emptying into the main aisle.

I don't do that on every flight. Only when I'm going home.

There is a leap of the heart as I exit the plane. I almost get nervous as I walk up the ramp. Most of the people see that I'm not the one they want and look past me. But from the side I hear the familiar shriek of two little girls. "Daddy!" Behind them I see a third face–little Sara, only a few months old. Deeply asleep, she furrows her brow slightly in reaction to the squealing. And then I see a fourth face–my wife's face. Faces of home.

That is what makes the promise at the end of the Beatitudes so compelling: "Rejoice and be glad, because great is your reward in heaven." What is our reward? Home.

The Book of Revelation could be entitled the Book of Homecoming, for in it we are given a picture of our heavenly home.

John's descriptions of the future steal your breath. His depiction of the final battle is graphic. Good clashes with evil. The sacred encounters the sinful. The pages howl with the shrieks of dragons and smolder with the coals of fiery pits. But in the midst of the battlefield there is a rose. John describes it in chapter 21: *"Then I saw a new heaven and a new earth...."*

John is old when he writes these words. His body is weary. The journey has taken its toll. His friends are gone. Peter is dead. Paul has been martyred. Andrew, James, Nathaniel . . . they are fuzzy figures from an early era. In this final mountaintop encounter, God pulls back the curtain and allows the warrior to peek into the homeland. When given the task of writing down what he sees, John chooses the most beautiful comparison earth has to offer. The Holy City, John says, is like *"a bride beautifully dressed for her husband."* When you look at this world, stained by innocent blood and smudged with selfishness, doesn't it make you want to go home?

The old saint tells us that when we get home, God himself will wipe away our tears. The same hands that stretched the heavens will touch your cheeks. The same hands that formed the mountains will caress your face. The same hands that curled in agony as the Roman spike cut through will someday cup your face and brush away your tears. Forever.

When you think of a world where there will be no reason to cry, ever, doesn't it make you want to go home?

"There will be no more death. . ." John declares. Can you imagine it? A world with no hearses or morgues or cemeteries or tombstones? Can you imagine a world with no spades of dirt thrown on caskets? No names chiseled into marble? No funerals? No black dresses? No black wreaths?

The hardest task in this world is to place a final kiss on cold lips that cannot kiss in return. The hardest thing in this world is to say goodbye. In the next world, John says, "goodbye" will never be spoken.

Tell me, doesn't that make you want to go home?

The most hopeful words of that passage from Revelation are those of God's resolve: "I am making everything new." It's hard to see things grow old. The town in which I grew up is growing old. I wish I could make it all new again. I wish I could blow the dust off the streets. I wish I could walk through the familiar neighborhood, and wave at the familiar faces, and pet the familiar dogs, and hit one more home run in the Little League park. I wish I could walk down Main Street and call out the merchants that have retired and open the doors that have been boarded up. I wish I could make everything new . . . but I can't.

I can't. But God can. He doesn't camouflage the old; he restores the new. The Master Builder will pull out the original plan and restore it. He will restore the vigor. He will restore the energy. He will restore the hope. He will restore the soul.

When you see how this world grows stooped and weary and then read of a home where everything is made new, tell me, doesn't that make you want to go home?

What would you give in exchange for a home like that? Would you really rather have a few possessions on earth than eternal possessions in heaven? Would you really choose a life of slavery to passion over a life of freedom? Would you honestly give up all of your heavenly mansions for a second-rate sleazy motel on earth?

I'll be home soon. The plane will land. I'll walk down that ramp and hear my name and see their faces. I'll be home soon.

You'll be home soon, too. You may not have noticed it, but you are closer to home than ever before. Each moment is a step taken. Each breath is a page turned. Each day is a mile marked, a mountain climbed. You are closer to home than you've ever been.

BETWEEN YOU AND GOD

Name the people and things that give you joy when you return home after many days away. How do they compare with the vision of the home John paints in Revelation?

_____

_____

_____

What would you like to say to the Lord?

_____

_____

_____

_____

_____

_____

_____

_____

_____

_____

_____

_____

_____

[1] Adapted from *The Applause of Heaven,* pp. 185-194.

A SATISFIED THIRST

MATTHEW 5:6
*Blessed are those who hunger and thirst for righteousness,
for they will be filled.*

"Mommy, I'm so thirsty. I want a drink."

Susanna Petroysan heard her daughter's pleas, but there was nothing she could do. She and four-year-old Gayaney were trapped beneath tons of collapsed concrete and steel. Beside them in the darkness lay the body of Susanna's sister-in-law, Karine, one of the fifty-five thousand victims of the worst earthquake in the history of Soviet Armenia.

Calamity never knocks before it enters, and this time, it had torn down the door.

Susanna had gone to Karine's house to try on a dress. It was December 7, 1998, at 11:30 A.M. The quake hit at 11:41. She had just removed the dress and was clad in stockings and a slip when the fifth-floor apartment began to shake. Susanna grabbed her daughter but had taken only a few steps before the floor opened up and they tumbled in. Susanna, Gayaney, and Karine fell into the basement with the nine-story apartment house crumbling around them.

"Mommy, I need a drink. Please give me something."

There was nothing for Susanna to give. She was trapped flat on her back. A concrete panel eighteen inches above her head and a crumpled water pipe above her shoulders kept her from standing. Feeling around in the darkness, she found a twenty-four-ounce jar of blackberry jam that had fallen into the basement. She gave the entire jar to her daughter to eat. It was gone by the second day.

"Mommy, I'm so thirsty."

Susanna knew she would die, but she wanted her daughter to live. She found a dress, perhaps the one she had come to try on, and made a bed for Gayaney. Though it was bitter cold, she took off her stockings and wrapped them around the child to keep her warm.

The two were trapped for eight days. Because of the darkness, Susanna lost track of time. Because of the cold, she lost the feeling in her fingers and toes. Because of her inability to move, she lost hope. "I was just waiting for death."

She began to hallucinate. Her thoughts wandered. A merciful sleep occasionally freed her from the horror of her entombment, but the sleep would be brief. Something always awakened her: the cold, the hunger, or–most often–the voice of her daughter.

"Mommy, I'm thirsty."

At some point in that eternal night, Susanna had an idea. She remembered a television program about an explorer in the Arctic who was dying of thirst. His comrade slashed open his hand and gave his friend his blood.

"I had no water, no fruit juice, no liquids. It was then I remembered I had my own blood."

Her groping fingers, numb from the cold, found a piece of shattered glass. She sliced open her left index finger and gave it to her daughter to suck. The drops of blood weren't enough.

"Please, Mommy, some more. Cut another finger." Susanna has no idea how many times she cut herself. She only knows that if she hadn't, Gayaney would have died. Her blood was her daughter's only hope.

++++++++++

"This cup is the new covenant in my blood," Jesus explained, holding up the wine.

The claim must have puzzled the apostles. They had been taught the story of the Passover wine. It symbolized the lamb's blood that the Israelites, enslaved long ago in Egypt, had painted on the doorposts of their homes. That blood had kept death from their homes and saved their firstborn. It had helped deliver them from the clutches of the Egyptians.

For thousands of generations the Jews had observed the Passover by sacrificing the lambs. Every year the blood would be poured, and every year the deliverance would be celebrated. The law called for spilling the blood of a lamb. That would be enough.

It would be enough to fulfill the law. It would be enough to satisfy the command. It would be enough to justify God's justice. But it would not be enough to take away sin. Sacrifices could offer temporary solutions, but only God could offer the eternal one. So he did.

Beneath the rubble of a fallen world, he pierced his hands. In the wreckage of a collapsed humanity, he ripped open his side. His children were trapped, so he gave his blood. It was all he had. His friends were gone. His strength was waning. His possessions had been gambled away at his feet. Even his Father had turned his head. His blood was all he had. But his blood was all it took.

"If anyone is thirsty," Jesus once said, "let him come to me and drink" (Jn. 7:37).

Admission of thirst doesn't come easy for us. False fountains pacify our cravings with sugary swallows of pleasure. But there comes a time when pleasure doesn't satisfy. There comes a dark hour in every life when the world caves in and we are left trapped in the rubble of reality, parched and dying. Some would rather die than admit it. Others admit it and escape death.

And we are very thirsty. Not thirsty for fame, possessions, passion, or romance. We've drunk from those pools. They are salt water in the desert. They don't quench–they kill. "Blessed are those who hunger and thirst for righteousness ...."

Righteousness. That's it. That's what we are thirsty for. We're thirsty for a clean conscience. We crave a clean slate. We yearn for a fresh start. We pray for a hand which will enter the dark cavern of our world and do for us the one thing we can't do for ourselves–make us right again.

+++++++++++++

"Mommy, I'm so thirsty," Gayaney begged.

"It was then I remembered I had my own blood," Susanna explained.

And the hand was cut, and the blood was poured, and the child was saved.

"God, I'm so thirsty," we pray.

"It is my blood, the blood of the new agreement," Jesus stated, "shed to set many free from their sins" (Mt. 26:28 Phillips).

And the hand was pierced, and the blood was poured, and the children are saved.[1]

BETWEEN YOU AND GOD

What are you thirsty for? A clean conscience, a clean slate, a fresh start?

_____

_____

_____

What would you like to say to the Lord?

_____

_____

_____

_____

_____

_____

_____

---

[1] *The Applause of Heaven*, pp. 93-98.

HE SPEAKS THROUGH THE STORM

JOB 42:5
My ears had heard of you but now my eyes have seen you.

It all happened in one day. One day he could choose his tee time at the nicest golf course in the country; the next he couldn't even be the caddie. One day he could Lear jet across the country to see the heavyweight bout at the Las Vegas Mirage. The next he couldn't afford a city bus across town.

Talk about calm becoming chaos . . . .

The first thing to go is his empire. The market crashes; his assets tumble. What is liquid goes dry. What has been up goes down. Stocks go flat, and Job goes broke. There he sits in his leather chair and soon-to-be-auctioned-off mahogany desk when the phone rings with news of calamity number two:

The kids were at a resort for the holidays when a storm blew in and took them with it.

Shell-shocked and dumbfounded, Job looks out the window into the sky that seems to be getting darker by the minute. He starts praying, telling God that things can't get any worse . . . and that's exactly what happens. He feels a pain in his chest that is more than last night's ravioli. The next thing he knows, he is bouncing in an ambulance with wires stuck to his chest and needles stuck in his arm.

He ends up tethered to a heart monitor in a community hospital room. Next to him lies an illegal immigrant who can't speak English.

Not, however, that Job lacks for conversation.

First there is his wife. Who could blame her for being upset at the week's calamities? Who could blame her for telling Job to curse God? But to curse God and die? If Job doesn't already feel abandoned, you know he does the minute his wife tells him to pull the plug and be done with it.

Then there are his friends. They have the bedside manner of a drill sergeant and the compassion of a chainsaw killer. A revised version of their theology might read like this: "Boy, you must have done something really bad! We know that God is good, so if bad things are happening to you, then you have been bad. Period."

"I'm not a bad man," Job argues. "I paid my taxes. I'm active in civic duties. I'm a major contributor to United Way and a volunteer at the hospital bazaar." Job is, in his eyes, a good man. And a good man, he reasons, deserves a good answer.

"Your suffering is for your own good," states Elihu, a young minister fresh out of seminary who hasn't lived long enough to be cynical and hasn't hurt enough to be quiet. He paces back and forth in the hospital room, with his Bible under his arm and his finger punching the air. What the young man says isn't bad theology, but it isn't much comfort, either.

Job steadily tunes him out and slides lower and lower under the covers. His head hurts. His eyes burn. His legs ache. And he can't stomach any more hollow homilies.

Yet his question still hasn't been answered: "God, why is this happening to me?"

So God speaks.

Out of the thunder, he speaks. Out of the sky, he speaks. For all of us who would put ditto marks under Job's question and sign our names to it, he speaks.

- For the father who holds a rose taken off his son's coffin, he speaks.
- For the wife who holds the flag taken off her husband's casket, he speaks.
- For the couple with the barren womb and the fervent prayers, he speaks.
- For any person who has tried to see God through shattered glass, he speaks.
- For those of us who have dared to say, "If God is God, then . . . ," God speaks.

He speaks out of the storm and into the storm, for that is where Job is. That is where God is best heard.
God's voice thunders in the room. Elihu sits down. Job sits up. And the two will never be the same again.

One question would have been enough for Job, but it isn't enough for God. Questions rush forth. They pour like sheets of rain out of the clouds. They splatter in the chambers of Job's heart with a wildness and a beauty and a terror that leave every Job who has ever lived drenched and speechless, watching the Master redefine who is who in the universe.

God's questions aren't intended to teach; they are intended to stun. They aren't intended to enlighten; they are intended to awaken. They aren't intended to stir the mind; they are intended to *bend the knees.*

God's message has connected: Job couldn't argue. God owes no one anything. No explanations. No excuses. No help. God has no debt, no outstanding balance, no favors to return. God owes no man anything. Which makes the fact that he gave us everything even more astounding.

How you interpret this holy presentation is key. You can interpret God's hammering speech as a divine "in-your-face" tirade if you want. You can use the list of unanswerable questions to prove that God is harsh, cruel, and distant. You can use the Book of Job as evidence that God gives us questions and no answers. But to do so, you need some scissors. To do so, you need to cut out the rest of the Book of Job.

For that is not how Job heard it. All his life, Job had been a good man. All his life, he had believed in God. All his life, he had discussed God, had notions about him, and had prayed to him.

But in the storm Job sees him! He sees Hope. Lover. Destroyer. Giver. Taker. Dreamer. Deliverer.

Job sees the tender anger of a God whose unending love is often received with peculiar mistrust. Job stands as a blade of grass against the consuming fire of God's splendor. Job's demands melt like wax as God pulls back the curtain and heaven's light falls uneclipsed across the earth.

Job sees God.

God could turn away at this point. The gavel has been slammed, the verdict has been rendered. The Eternal Judge has spoken.

Ah, but God is not angry with Job. Firm? Yes. Direct? No doubt. Clear and convincing? Absolutely. But angry? No. God is never irritated by the candle of an honest seeker.

Job sees God–and that is enough. But it isn't enough for God.

The years to come find Job once again sitting behind his mahogany desk with health restored and profits up. His lap is once again full of children and grandchildren and great-grandchildren–for four generations! If Job ever wonders why God doesn't bring back the children he had taken away, he doesn't ask. Maybe he doesn't ask because he knows that his children could never be happier than they are in the presence of this One he has seen so briefly.

Something tells me that Job would do it all again, if that's what it took to hear God's voice and stand in the Presence. Even if God left him with his bedsores and bills, Job would do it again.

For God gave Job more than Job ever dreamed. God gave Job Himself.[1]

BETWEEN YOU AND GOD

How did you interpret God's message to Job previously? Has your view changed after reading this meditation?

_____

_____

What would you like to say to the Lord?

_____

_____

_____

_____

_____

_____

_____

---

[1] Adapted from *In the Eye of the Storm*, pp. 185-187.

COME AND SEE

JOHN 1:45-46
Philip found Nathanael and told him, "We have found the one Moses wrote about in the Law, and about whom the prophets also wrote–Jesus of Nazareth, the son of Joseph."
"Nazareth! Can anything good come from there?" Nathanael asked.
"Come and see," said Philip.

The first answer given the first doubter is the only one necessary. When Nathanael doubted that anything good could come out of Nazareth, Philip's response was simply, "Come and see."

Nathanael's question remains: "Can anything good come out of Nazareth?" Have two thousand years of Christianity changed this world? Is the life of the young Nazarene carpenter really worth considering? The question still lingers. And the answer of Philip still suffices. Come and see.

Come and see the rock that has withstood the winds of time. Hear his voice.
The truth undaunted, grace unspotted, loyalty undeterred.
Come and see the flame that tyrants and despots have not extinguished.
Come and see the passion that oppression has not squelched.
Come and see the hospitals and orphanages rising beside the crumbling ruins of humanism and atheism.
Come and see what Christ has done.

Come and see the great drama threading through twenty centuries of history and art.
Handel weeping as he composes *The Messiah.*
Da Vinci sighing as he portrays the Last Supper.
Michelangelo stepping back from the rock-carved David and bidding the stone to speak.

Can anything good come out of Nazareth? Come and see.
See Wilberforce fighting to free slaves in England—because he believed.
See Washington at prayer in Valley Forge–because he believed.
See Lincoln alone with a dog-eared Bible–because he believed.

Come and see the changed lives: the alcoholic now dry, the embittered now joyful, the shamed now forgiven. Come and see the marriages rebuilt, the orphans embraced, the imprisoned inspired. Journey into the jungles and hear the drums beating in praise. Sneak into the corners of communism and find believers worshiping under threat of death.

Walk on death row and witness the prisoner condemned by man yet liberated by God. Venture into the gulags and dungeons of the world and hear the songs of the saved refusing to be silent.

Can anything good come out of Nazareth? Come and see the pierced hand of God touch the most common heart, wipe the tear from the wrinkled face, and forgive the ugliest sin.

Come and see.
Come and see the tomb. The tomb once occupied, now vacant; the grave once sealed, now empty. Cynics have raised their theories, doubters have raised their questions. But their musings continue to melt in the bright light of Easter morning.

Come and see. He avoids no seeker. He ignores no probe. He fears no search. Come and see. Nathanael came. And Nathanael saw. And Nathanael discovered, "Teacher, you are the Son of God; you are the King of Israel" (NCV)[1].

---

[1] Adapted from *A Gentle Thunder,* pp. 21-23.

BETWEEN YOU AND GOD

Have you seen Jesus' power touch the heart of someone you love? Have you personally experienced his hand of comfort in a time of great sorrow? Do you believe he lives today as surely as he walked the shores of Galilee?

_____

_____

_____

What would you like to say to the Lord?

_____

_____

_____

_____

_____

_____

_____

_____

_____

_____

_____

_____

_____

_____

_____

_____

THE GIFT OF UNHAPPINESS

ECCLESIASTES 3:11A
He has made everything beautiful in its time. He has also set eternity in the hearts of men.
1 CORINTHIANS 2:9
"No eye has seen, no ear has heard, no mind has conceived what God has prepared for those who love him."

There dwells inside you, deep within, a tiny whippoorwill. Listen. You will hear him sing. His aria mourns the dusk. His solo signals the dawn.

It is the song of the whippoorwill.

He will not be silent until the sun is seen.

We forget he is there, so easy is he to ignore. Other animals of the heart are larger, noisier, more demanding, more imposing. But none is so constant.

Other creatures of the soul are more quickly fed. More simply satisfied. We feed the lion who growls for power. We stroke the tiger who demands affection. We bridle the stallion who bucks control. But what do we do with the whippoorwill who yearns for eternity?

For that is his song. That is his task. Out of the gray he sings a golden song. Perched in time he chirps a timeless verse. Peering through pain's shroud, he sees a painless place. Of that place he sings. And though we try to ignore him, we cannot. He is us, and his song is ours. Our heart song won't be silenced until we see the dawn.

"God has planted eternity in the hearts of men" (Eccles. 3:11 TLB), says the wise man. But it doesn't take a wise person to know that people long for more than earth. When we see pain, we yearn. When we see hunger, we question why. Senseless deaths. Endless tears. Needless loss. Where do they come from? Where will they lead? Isn't there more to life than death? And so sings the whippoorwill.

We try to quiet this terrible, tiny voice. Like a parent hushing a child, we place a finger over puckered lips and request silence. *I'm too busy now to talk. I'm too busy to think. I'm too busy to question.* And so we busy ourselves with the task of staying busy. But occasionally we hear his song. And occasionally we let the song whisper to us that there is something more. There *must* be something more.

And as long as we hear the song, we are comforted. As long as we are discontent, we will search. As long as we know there is a far-off country, we will have hope.

The only ultimate disaster that can befall us, I have come to realize, is to feel ourselves to be home on earth. As long as we are aliens, we cannot forget our true homeland. Unhappiness on earth cultivates a hunger for heaven. By gracing us with a deep dissatisfaction, God holds our attention. The only tragedy, then, is to be satisfied prematurely. To settle for earth. To be content in a strange land. To intermarry with the Babylonians and forget Jerusalem.

We are not happy here because we are not at home here. We are not happy here because we are not supposed to be happy here. We are *"like foreigners and strangers in this world"* (1 Pet. 2:11).

Take a fish and place him on the beach. Watch his gills gasp and scales dry. Is he happy? No! How do you make him happy? Do you cover him with a mountain of cash? Do you get him a beach chair and sunglasses? Do you bring him a *Playfish* magazine and martini? Do you wardrobe him in double-breasted fins and people-skinned shoes?

Of course not. Then how do you make him happy? You put him back in his element. You put him back in the water. He will never be happy on the beach simply because he was not made for the beach.

And you will never be completely happy on earth simply because you were not made for earth. Oh, you will have your moments of joy. You will catch glimpses of light. You will know moments or even days of peace. But they simply do not compare with the happiness that lies ahead.

Rest on this earth is a false rest. Beware of those who urge you to find happiness here; you won't find it. Guard against the false physicians who promise that joy is only a diet away, a marriage away, a job away, or a transfer away. The prophet denounced people like this: *"They tried to heal my people's serious injuries as if they were small wounds. They said, 'It's all right, it's all right.' But really, it is not all right"* (Jer. 6:14 NCV).

And it won't be all right until we get home.

Again, we have our moments. The newborn on our breast, the bride on our arm, the sunshine on our back. But even those moments are simply slivers of light breaking through heaven's window. God flirts with us. He tantalizes us. He romances us. Those moments are appetizers for the dish that is to come. *Heaven is beyond our imagination.* We cannot envision it. At our most creative moment, at our deepest thought, at our highest level, we still cannot fathom eternity.

Try this. Imagine a perfect world. Whatever that means to you, imagine it. Does that mean peace? Then envision absolute tranquility. Does a perfect world imply joy? Then create your highest happiness. Will a perfect world have love? If so, ponder a place where love has no bounds. Whatever heaven means to you, imagine it. Get it firmly fixed in your mind. Delight in it. Dream about it. Long for it.

And then smile as the Father reminds you, *No one has ever imagined what God has prepared for those who love him.* Anything you imagine is inadequate. Anything anyone imagines is inadequate. No one has come close. No one. Think of all the songs about heaven. All the artists' portrayals. All the lessons preached, poems written, and chapters drafted.

When it comes to describing heaven, we are all happy failures. It's beyond us.

But it's also within us. The song of the whippoorwill. Let her sing. Let her sing in the dark. Let her sing at the dawn. Let her song remind you that you were not made for this place and that there is a place made just for you.

But until then, be realistic. Lower your expectations of earth. This is not heaven, so don't expect it to be. There will never be a newscast with no bad news. There will never be a church with no gossip or competition. There will never be a new car, new wife, or new baby who can give you the joy your heart craves. Only God can.

And God will. Be patient. And be listening. Listening for the song of the whippoorwill.[1]

BETWEEN YOU AND GOD

Have you expected too much of happiness on this earth? If so, what has been the result? If not, why not?

_____

_____

_____

What would you like to say to the Lord?

_____

_____

_____

_____

_____

_____

_____

_____

_____

_____

---

[1] *When God Whispers Your Name,* pp.165-169.

Notes – Week Three

FACE TO FACE
PRE-RETREAT DEVOTIONAL

Week Four
God's Call

THE CHOICE

Genesis 1:27
So God created man in his own image, in the image of God he created him; male and female he created them.

He placed one scoop of clay upon another until a form lay lifeless on the ground.

All of the Garden's inhabitants paused to witness the event. Hawks hovered. Giraffes stretched. Trees bowed. Butterflies paused on petals and watched.

"You will love me, nature," God said. "I made you that way. You will obey me, universe. For you were designed to do so. You will reflect my glory, skies, for that is how you were created. But this one will be like me. This one will be able to choose."

All were silent as the Creator reached into himself and removed something yet unseen. A seed. "It's called 'choice.' The seed of choice."

Creation stood in silence and gazed upon the lifeless form.

An angel spoke, "But what if he . . . ."

"What if he chooses not to love?" the Creator finished. "Come, I will show you."

Unbound by today, God and the angel walked into the realm of tomorrow.

"There, see the fruit of the seed of choice, both the sweet and the bitter."

The angel gasped at what he saw. Spontaneous love. Voluntary devotion. Chosen tenderness. Never had he seen anything like these. He felt the love of the Adams. He heard the joy of Eve and her daughters. He saw the food and the burdens shared. He absorbed the kindness and marveled at the warmth.

"Heaven has never seen such beauty, my Lord. Truly, this is your greatest creation."

"Ah, but you've only seen the sweet. Now witness the bitter."

A stench enveloped the pair. The angel turned in horror and proclaimed, "What is it?"

The Creator spoke only one word: "Selfishness."

The angel stood speechless as they passed through centuries of repugnance. Never had he seen such filth. Rotten hearts. Ruptured promises. Forgotten loyalties. Children of the creation wandering blindly in lonely labyrinths.

"This is the result of choice?" the angel asked.

"Yes."

"They will forget you?"

"Yes."

"They will reject you?"

"Yes."

"They will never come back?"

"Some will. Most won't."

"What will it take to make them listen?"

The Creator walked on in time, further and further into the future, until he stood by a tree. A tree that would be fashioned into a cradle. Even then he could smell the hay that would surround him.

With another step into the future, he paused before another tree. It stood alone, a stubborn ruler of a bald hill. The trunk was thick, and the wood vas strong. Soon it would be cut. Soon it would be trimmed. Soon it would be mounted on the stony brow of another hill. And soon he would be hung on it.

He felt the wood rub against a back he did not yet wear.

"Will you go down there?" the angel asked.

"I will."

"Is there no other way?"

"There is not."

"Wouldn't it be easier to not plant the seed? Wouldn't it be easier to not give the choice?"

"It would," the Creator spoke slowly. "But to remove the choice is to remove the love."

He looked around the hill and foresaw a scene. Three figures hung on three crosses. Arms spread. Heads fallen forward. They moaned with the wind.

Men clad in soldiers' garb sat on the ground near the trio. They played games in the dirt and laughed.

Men clad in religion stood off to one side. They smiled. Arrogant, cocky. They had protected God, they thought, by killing this false one.

Women clad in sorrow huddled at the foot of the hill. Speechless. Faces tear streaked. Eyes downward. One put her arm around another and tried to lead her away. She wouldn't leave. "I will stay," she said softly. "I will stay."

All heaven stood to fight. All nature rose to rescue. All eternity poised to protect. But the Creator gave no command.

"It must be done . . . ," he said, and withdrew.

But as he stepped back in time, he heard the cry that he would someday scream: "My God, my God, why have you forsaken me?" He wrenched at tomorrow's agony.

The angel spoke again. "It would be less painful . . ."

The Creator interrupted softly. "But it wouldn't be love."

They stepped into the Garden again. The Maker looked earnestly at the clay creation. A monsoon of love swelled up within him. He had died for the creation before he had made him. God's form bent over the sculptured face and breathed. Dust stirred on the lips of the new one. The chest rose, cracking the red mud. The cheeks fleshened. A finger moved. And an eye opened.

But more incredible than the moving of the flesh was the stirring of the spirit. Those who could see the unseen gasped.

Perhaps it was the wind who said it first. Perhaps what the star saw that moment is what has made it blink ever since. Maybe it was left to an angel to whisper it:

"It looks like . . . it appears so much like . . . it is him!"

The angel wasn't speaking of the face, the features, or the body. He was looking inside—at the soul.

"It's eternal!" gasped another.

Within the man, God had placed a divine seed. A seed of his self. The God of might had created earth's mightiest. The Creator had created, not a creature, but another creator. And the One who had chosen to love had created one who could love in return.

Now it's our choice.[1]

BETWEEN YOU AND GOD

How have you used your freedom to choose—for the better or the worse?

_____

_____

_____

What would you like to say to the Lord?

_____

_____

_____

_____

_____

_____

_____

_____

---

[1] *In the Eye of the Storm*, pp. 237-243.

THE YAY-YUCK MAN

Romans 12:2
Do not conform any longer to the pattern of this world, but be transformed by the renewing of your mind. Then you will be able to test and approve what God's will is—his good, pleasing and perfect will.

Bob loved to make people happy. Bob lived to make people happy.

If people weren't happy, Bob wasn't happy. So every day Bob set out to make people happy. Not an easy task, for what makes some people happy makes other people angry.

Bob lived in a land where everyone wore coats. The people never removed their coats. Bob never asked *Why?* He only asked *Which?* "Which coat should I wear?"

Bob's mother loved blue. So to please her he wore a blue coat. When she would see him wearing blue she would say, "Yay, Bob! I love it when you wear blue." So he wore the blue coat all the time. And since he never left his house and since he saw no one but his mother, he was happy, for she was happy and she said "Yay, Bob" over and over.

Bob grew up and got a job. The first day of his first job he got up early and put on his best blue coat and walked down the street.

The crowds on the street, however, didn't like blue. They liked green. Everyone on the street wore green. As he walked past, everyone looked at his blue coat and said, "Yuck!"

Yuck! was a hard word for Bob to hear. When the people saw his blue coat and said "yuck," Bob dashed into a clothing store and bought a green coat. He put it on over his blue coat and walked back out in the street. "Yay! " the people shouted as he walked past. He felt better because he had made them feel better.

When he arrived at his workplace, he walked into his boss's office wearing a green coat. "Yuck!" said his boss.

"Oh, I'm sorry," said Bob, quickly removing the green coat and revealing the blue. "You must be like my mother."

"Double yuck!" responded the boss. He got up from his chair, walked to the closet, and produced a yellow coat. "We like yellow here," he instructed.

"Whatever you say, sir," Bob answered, relieved to know he wouldn't have to hear his boss say "yuck" anymore. He put the yellow coat over the green coat, which was over the blue coat. And so he went to work.

When it was time for him to go home, he replaced the yellow coat with the green and walked through the streets. Just before he got to his house, he put the blue coat over the green and yellow coats and went inside.

Bob learned that life with three coats was hard. His movements were stiff, and he was always hot. There were also times when the cuff of one coat would peek out and someone would notice, but before the person could say "yuck" Bob would tuck it away.

One day he forgot to change his coat before he went home, and when his mother saw green she turned purple with disgust and started to say, "Yuck." But before she could, Bob ran and put his hand on her mouth and held the word in while he traded coats and then removed his hand so she said, "Yay!"

It was at this moment that Bob realized he had a special gift. He could change his colors with ease. With a little practice, he was able to shed one coat and replace it with another in a matter of seconds.

His skill at changing coats quickly elevated him to high positions. Everyone liked him because everyone thought he was just like them. With time he was elected mayor over the entire city.

His acceptance speech was brilliant. Those who loved green thought he was wearing green. Those who loved yellow thought he was wearing yellow, and his mother just knew he was wearing blue. Only he knew that he was constantly changing from one to the other.

It wasn't easy, but it was worth it, because at the end everyone said, "Yay!"

Bob's multicolored life continued until one day some yellowcoated people stormed into his office. "We have found a criminal who needs to be executed," they announced, shoving a man toward Bob's desk. Bob was shocked at what he saw. The man wasn't wearing a coat at all, just a T-shirt.

"Leave him with me," Bob instructed, and the yellow coats left.

"Where is your coat?" asked the mayor.

"I don't wear one."

"You don't have one?"

"I don't want one."

"You don't want a coat? But everyone wears a coat. It, it, it's the way things are here."

"I'm not from here."

"What coat do they wear where you are from?"

"No coat."

"None?"

"None."

Bob looked at the man with amazement. "But what if people don't approve?"

"It's not their approval I seek. I am here to show people they don't have to please people. I am here to tell the truth."

If Bob had ever heard of the word truth, he'd long since rejected it. "What is truth?" he asked.

But before the man could answer, people outside the mayor's office began to scream, "Kill him! Kill him!"

A mob had gathered outside the window. Bob went to it and saw the crowd was wearing green. Putting on his green coat, he said, "There is nothing wrong with this man."

"Yuck!" they shouted. Bob fell back at the sound.

By then the yellow coats were back in his office. Seeing them, Bob changed his colors and pleaded, "The man is innocent."

"Yuck!" they proclaimed. Bob covered his ears at the word.

He looked at the man and pleaded, "Who are you?"

The man answered simply, "Who are you?"

Bob did not know. But suddenly he wanted to. Just then his mother, who'd heard of the crisis, entered the office. Without realizing it, Bob changed to blue. "He is not one of us," she said.

"But, but, . . ."

"Kill him!"

A torrent of voices came from all directions. Bob again covered his ears and looked at the man with no coat. The man was silent. Bob was tormented. "I can't please them and set you free!" he shouted over their screams.

The man with no coat was silent.

"I can't please you and them!"

Still the man was silent.

"Speak to me!" Bob demanded.

The man with no coat spoke one word. "Choose."

"I can't!" Bob declared. He threw up his hands and screamed, "Take him, I wash my hands of the choice."

But even Bob knew in making no choice he had made one. The man was led away, and Bob was left alone. Alone with his coats.[1]

BETWEEN YOU AND GOD

What choice have you made—pleasing people or pleasing God? Why?

_____

_____

_____

What would you like to say to the Lord?

_____

_____

_____

---

[1] *A Gentle Thunder*, pp. 113-116.

FENDING OFF THE VOICES

JOHN 10:2-5
The man who enters by the gate is the shepherd of his sheep. The watchman opens the gate for him, and the sheep listen to his voice. He calls his own sheep by name and leads them out. When he has brought out all his own, he goes on ahead of them, and his sheep follow him because they know his voice. But they will never follow a stranger; in fact, they will run away from him because they do not recognize a stranger's voice.

"After the people saw the miraculous sign that Jesus did, they began to say, `Surely this is the Prophet who is to come into the world.'"

"Jesus, knowing that they intended to come and make him king by force, withdrew again to a mountain by himself.

You've heard the lying voices that noise our world. They tell you to swap your integrity for a new sale. To barter your convictions for an easy deal. To exchange your devotion for a quick thrill.

They whisper. They woo. They taunt. They tantalize. They flirt. They flatter. "Go ahead, it's OK." "Just wait until tomorrow." "Don't worry, no one will know." "How could anything that feels so right be so wrong?"

A placard on my nightstand invites me to a lounge in the lobby, where I can "make new friends in a relaxing atmosphere." An advertisement on top of the television promises me that with the request of a late-night adult movie my "fantasies will come true." In the phone book, several columns of escort services offer "love away from home." An attractive, gold-lettered volume in the drawer of the nightstand beckons: *The Book of Mormon: Another Testament of Jesus Christ.* On television a talk-show host discusses the day's topic: "How to succeed at sex in the office."

Voices. Some for pleasure. Some for power.

Some promise acceptance. Some promise tenderness. But all promise something.

And don't think for a minute that Christ didn't hear their chant.

A chorus promising power intoxicates. No cross needed. No sacrifice required. An army of disciples at his fingertips. Power to change the world without having to die doing it.

Yes, Jesus heard the voices. He heard the lurings. But he also heard someone else.

And when Jesus heard him, he sought him.

Jesus preferred to be alone with the true God rather than in a crowd with the wrong people.

Logic didn't tell him to dismiss the crowds. Conventional wisdom didn't tell him to turn his back on a willing army. No, it wasn't a voice from without that Jesus heard. It was a voice from within.

The mark of a disciple is his or her ability to hear the Master's voice.

"Here I am! I stand at the door and knock. If anyone hears my voice and opens the door, I will come in and eat with him, and he with me" (Rev. 3:20).

The world rams at your door; Jesus taps at your door. The voices scream for your allegiance; Jesus softly and tenderly requests it. The world promises flashy pleasure;

Jesus promises a quiet dinner . . . with God. "I will come in and eat."

Which voice do you hear?

Let me state something important. There is never a time during which Jesus is not speaking. Never. There is never a place in which Jesus is not present. Never. There is never a room so dark . . . a lounge so sensual . . . an office so sophisticated . . . that the ever-present, ever-pursuing, relentlessly tender Friend is not there, tapping gently on the doors of our hearts-waiting to be invited in.

Few hear his voice. Fewer still open the door.

But never interpret our numbness as his absence. For amidst the fleeting promises of pleasure is the timeless promise of his presence. "Surely I am with you always, to the very end of the age" (Mt. 28:20).

There is no chorus so loud that the voice of God cannot be heard . . . if we will but listen.

That's true in this hotel room.

It took me a few minutes to find it, but I did. It wasn't as visible as the lounge placard or the movie advertisement. But it was there. It wasn't as fancy as the Mormon Bible or as attention-grabbing as the escort ads. But I'd give up those lies every time for the peace I've found in this treasure.

A Bible. A simple, hard-covered, Gideon-placed, King James Version Bible. It took me a few minutes to find it, but I did. And when I did, I opened it to one of my favorite voice passages:

> A time is coming when all who are in their graves will
> hear his voice and come out–those who have done
> good will rise to live, and those who have done evil
> will rise to be condemned.

Interesting. A day is coming when everyone will hear his voice. A day is coming when all the other voices will be silenced; his voice–and his voice only–will be heard.

Some will hear his voice for the very first time. It's not that he never spoke, it's just that they never listened. For these, God's voice will be the voice of a stranger. They will hear it once–and never hear it again. They will spend eternity fending off the voices they followed on earth.

But others will be called from their graves by a familiar voice. For they are sheep who know their shepherd. They are servants who opened the door when Jesus knocked.

Now the door will open again. Only this time, it won't be Jesus who walks into our house; it will be we, who walk into his.[1]

BETWEEN YOU AND GOD

Where are you when the voices of the world seem more compelling than the voice of God? At the office? Out with friends? Dancing with your girlfriend? Disciplining your child? Other?

_____

_____

_____

What would you like to say to the Lord?

_____

_____

_____

_____

_____

_____

_____

_____

_____

_____

_____

_____

_____

[1] *In the Eye of the Storm*, pp. 87-92.

OVERCOMING YOUR HERITAGE

GALATIANS 4:7
So you are no longer a slave, but a son; and since you are a son, God has made you also an heir.

Stefan can tell you about family trees. He makes his living from them. He inherited a German forest that has been in his family for 400 years. The trees he harvests were planted 180 years ago by his great-grandfather. The trees he plants won't be ready for market until his great-grandchildren are born.

He's part of a chain.

"Every generation must make a choice," he told me. "They can either pillage or plant. They can rape the landscape and get rich, or they can care for the landscape, harvest only what is theirs, and leave an investment for their children."

Stefan harvests seeds sown by men he never knew.

Stefan sows seeds to be harvested by descendants he'll never see.

Dependent upon the past, responsible for the future; he's part of a chain.

Like us. Children of the past, are we. Parents of the future. Heirs. Benefactors. Recipients of the work done by those before. Born into a forest we didn't seed.

Which leads me to ask, how's your forest?

As you stand on the land bequeathed by your ancestors, how does it look? How do you feel?

Pride at legacy left? Perhaps. Some inherit nourished soil. Deeply rooted trees of conviction. Row after row of truth and heritage. Could be that you stand in the forest of your fathers with pride. If so, give thanks, for many don't.

Many aren't proud of their family trees. Poverty. Shame. Abuse. Such are the forests found by some of you. The land was pillaged. Harvest was taken, but no seed was sown.

Perhaps you were reared in a home of bigotry and so you are intolerant of minorities. Perhaps you were reared in a home of greed, hence your desires for possessions are insatiable.

Perhaps your childhood memories bring more hurt than inspiration. The voices of your past cursed you, belittled you, ignored you. At the time, you thought such treatment was typical. Now you see it isn't.

Maybe your past isn't much to brag about. Maybe you've seen raw evil. And now you have to make a choice. Do you rise above the past and make a difference? Or do you remain controlled by the past and make excuses? Many choose the latter.

Many choose the convalescent homes of the heart. Healthy bodies. Sharp minds. But retired dreams. Back and forth they rock in the chair of regret, repeating the terms of surrender. Lean closely and you will hear them: "If only." The white flag of the heart.

"If only. . . ."

"If only I'd been born somewhere else . . . ."

"If only I'd been treated fairly . . . ."

"If only I'd had kinder parents, more money, greater opportunities . . . ."

Maybe you've used those words. Maybe you have every right to use them. Perhaps you were hearing the ten count before you even got into the ring. If such is the case, let me show you where to turn. Put down the scrapbook and pick up your Bible. Go to John's gospel and read Jesus' words: "Human life comes from human parents, but spiritual life comes from the Spirit" (John 3:6).

Think about that. Spiritual life comes from the Spirit! Your parents may have given you genes, but God gives you grace. Your parents may be responsible for your body, but God has taken charge of your soul. You may get your looks from your mother, but you get eternity from your Father, your heavenly Father.

By the way, he's not blind to your problems. In fact, God is willing to give you what your family didn't.

Didn't have a good father? He'll be your Father (Gal. 4:7).

Didn't have a good role model? Try God (Eph. 5:1).

Never had a parent who wiped away your tears? Think again. God has noted each one (Ps. 56:8).

God has not left you adrift on a sea of heredity. You cannot control the way your forefathers responded to God. But you can control the way you respond to him. The past does not have to be your prison. You have a voice in your destiny. You have a say in your life. You have a choice in the path you take.

Choose well and someday—generations from now—your grandchildren and great-grandchildren will thank God for the seeds you sowed.[1]

BETWEEN YOU AND GOD

Was your family heritage helpful or hurtful? In what way?

_____

_____

_____

What would you like your heritage to be for your children? Your grandchildren?

_____

_____

_____

_____

_____

What would you like to say to the Lord?

_____

_____

_____

_____

_____

_____

_____

_____

_____

_____

_____

_____

_____

[1] *When God Whispers Your Name*, pp. 97-104.

HIDDEN HEROES

LUKE 7:20
When the men came to Jesus, they said, "John the Baptist sent us to you to ask, 'Are you the one who was to come, or should we expect someone else?' "

True heroes are hard to identify. They don't look like heroes. Here's an example.

Step with me into a dank dungeon in Judea. Peer through the door's tiny window. Consider the plight of the man on the floor. He has just inaugurated history's greatest movement. His words have triggered a revolution that will span two millenniums. Future historians will describe him as courageous, noble, and visionary.

At this moment he appears anything but. Cheeks hollow. Beard matted. Bewilderment etched on his face. He leans back against the cold wall, closes his eyes, and sighs.

John had never known doubt. Hunger, yes. Loneliness, often. But doubt? Never. Only raw conviction, ruthless pronouncements, and rugged truth. Such was John the Baptist. Conviction as fierce as the desert sun.

Until now. Now the sun is blocked. Now his courage wanes. Now the clouds come. And now, as he faces death, he doesn't raise a fist of victory; he raises only a question. His final act is not a proclamation of courage, but a confession of confusion: "Find out if Jesus is the Son of God or not."

The forerunner of the Messiah is afraid of failure. *Find out if I've told the truth. Find out if I've sent people to the right Messiah. Find out if I've been right or if I've been duped.*

Doesn't sound too heroic, does he?

We'd rather John die in peace. We'd rather the trailblazer catch a glimpse of the mountain. Seems only right that the sailor be granted a sighting of the shore. After all, didn't Moses get a view of the valley? Isn't John the cousin of Jesus? If anybody deserves to see the end of the trail, doesn't he?

Apparently not.

The miracles he prophesied, he never saw. The kingdom he announced, he never knew. And the Messiah he proclaimed, he now doubts.

John doesn't look like the prophet who would be the transition between law and grace. He doesn't look like a hero.

Heroes seldom do.

For that reason, a hero could be next door and you wouldn't know it. The fellow who changes the oil in your car could be one. A hero in coveralls? Maybe. Maybe as he works he prays, asking God to do with the heart of the driver what he does with the engine.

The day-care worker where you drop off the kids? Perhaps. Perhaps her morning prayers include the name of each child and the dream that one of them will change the world. Who's to say God isn't listening?

The parole officer downtown? Could be a hero. She could be the one who challenges the ex-con to challenge the teens to challenge the gangs.

I know, I know. These folks don't fit our image of a hero. They look too, too, . . . well, normal. Give us four stars, titles, and headlines. But something tells me that for every hero in the spotlight, there are dozens in the shadows. They don't get press. They don't draw crowds. They don't even write books!

But behind every avalanche is a snowflake.

Behind a rock slide is a pebble.

An atomic explosion begins with one atom.

And a revival can begin with one sermon.

History proves it. John Egglen had never preached a sermon in his life. Never.

Wasn't that he didn't want to, just never needed to. But then one morning he did. The snow left his town of Colchester, England, buried in white. When he awoke on that January Sunday in 1850, he thought of staying home. Who would go to church in such weather?

But he reconsidered. He was, after all, a deacon. And if the deacons didn't go, who would? So he put on his boots, hat, and coat and walked the six miles to the Methodist Church.

He wasn't the only member who considered staying home. In fact, he was one of the few who came. Only thirteen people were present. Twelve members and one visitor. Even the minister was snowed in. Someone suggested they go home. Egglen would hear none of that. They'd come this far; they would have a service. Besides, they had a visitor. A thirteen-year-old boy.

But who would preach? Egglen was the only deacon. It fell to him.

And so he did. His sermon lasted only ten minutes. It drifted and wandered and made no point in an effort to make several. But at the end, an uncharacteristic courage settled upon the man. He lifted his eyes and looked straight at the boy and challenged: "Young man, look to Jesus. Look! Look! Look!"

Did the challenge make a difference? Let the boy, now a man, answer. "I did look, and then and there the cloud on my heart lifted, the darkness rolled away, and at that moment I saw the sun."

The boy's name? Charles Haddon Spurgeon. England's prince of preachers.

Did Egglen know what he'd done? No.

Do heroes know when they are heroic? Rarely.

Are historic moments acknowledged when they happen?

You know the answer to that one. (If not, a visit to the manger will remind you.) We seldom see history in the making, and we seldom recognize heroes. Which is just as well, for if we knew either, we might mess up both.

But we'd do well to keep our eyes open. Tomorrow's Spurgeon might be mowing your lawn. And the hero who inspires him might be nearer than you think.

He might be in your mirror.[1]

BETWEEN YOU AND GOD

What does a hero in God's eyes look like?

_____

_____

_____

What would you like to say to the Lord?

_____

_____

_____

_____

_____

_____

_____

_____

_____

_____

_____

_____

_____

_____

---

[1] Adapted from *When God Whispers Your Name*, pp. 27-33.

READY FOR HOME

GALATIANS 5:22-25
But the fruit of the Spirit is love, joy, peace, patience, kindness, goodness, faithfulness, gentleness and self-control. Against such things there is no law. Those who belong to Christ Jesus have crucified the sinful nature with its passions and desires. Since we live by the Spirit, let us keep in step with the Spirit.

Had you been on the British Coast in 1895 you might have seen two ships boarded by 138 of England's finest sailors setting sail for the Arctic. Their task? To chart the Northwest Passage around the Canadian Arctic to the Pacific Ocean.

The captain, Sir John Franklin, hoped this effort would be the turning point in Arctic exploration. History shows that it was. Not because of its success, but because of its failure. The ships never returned. Every crew member perished. And those who followed in the expedition's path to the pole learned this lesson: Prepare for the journey.

Apparently Franklin didn't. Though the voyage was projected to last two or three years, he only carried a twelve-day supply of coal for the auxiliary steam engines. But what he lacked in fuel, he made up for in entertainment. Each ship carried a "1,200 volume library, a hand-organ, china place settings for officers and men, cut-glass wine goblets and sterling silver flatware."[1]

Was the crew planning for an Arctic expedition or a Caribbean cruise? Judging from the supplies, one would have thought the latter. The sailors carried no special clothing to protect them against the cold. Only the uniforms of Her Majesty's fleet. Noble and respectful, but thin and inadequate.

The silver knives, forks, and spoons were as ornate as those found in the dining rooms of the Royal Navy officers clubs: heavy at the handles, intricately designed. Years later, some of these place settings would be found near a clump of frozen, cannibalized bodies.

The inevitable had occurred. The two ships had sailed ill-prepared into the frigid waters. Ice coated the deck, the spars, and the rigging. The sea froze around the rudder and trapped the ship.

The sailors set out to search for help, wearing their uniforms and carrying their belongings. Inuit Indians reported seeing a group dragging a wooden boat across the ice. For the next twenty years, remains of the expedition were found all over the frozen sea. The boat, or a similar one, was later discovered containing the bodies of thirty-five men. Other Indians discovered a tent on the ice and in it, thirty bodies.

Franklin died on the boat. Search parties would later find a piece of the backgammon board Lady Jane Franklin had given her husband as a farewell present.

Strange how men could embark on such a journey ill-prepared, more equipped for afternoon tea than for the open sea.

Stranger still how we do the same. Don't Franklin's men remind you of us? We sometimes act as if the Christian life is a retirement cruise. We have little fuel but lots of entertainment. We are more concerned with looking snappy than with being prepared. We give more thought to table settings than to surviving the journey. We give little thought to the destination, but we make sure there's plenty of silver to go around.

And so when the freeze comes, we step out on the ice with forks, games, and skimpy clothing and pass our final days walking against the wind, often blaming God for getting us into this mess.

But God is not to blame. If we sail unprepared it's in spite of—not because of–God. He left detailed instructions about this voyage. His Word is our map; the Holy Spirit is our compass.

He outlined the route and described the landmarks we should seek.

He even told us what to pack for the trip: love, joy, peace, patience, kindness, goodness, faithfulness, gentleness, self-control (see Gal. 5:22-23).

And most remarkably, he's gone before us and goes with us. He's both a pioneer and a co-traveler! And when we grow weary, all we need to do is listen to his voice. He's got special promises to keep us on the journey.

What fear strikes a man when the end is near and he's not prepared.

What fear must have struck the crew of Sir John Franklin when they became stuck in the ice. What anxiety to search for food and find silver, to dig in the closets for coats and find uniforms, to explore the ship for picks and axes and find backgammon games and novels.

Don't you know they would have swapped it all in a heartbeat for what they needed to get home safely?

By the way, what supplies are you taking? Are you carrying your share of silver and games? Don't be fooled; they may matter here, but they matter not when you reach your Father's house. What matters is if you are known by the Father.

It's not what you have; it's who you know. Be prepared. You don't want to be left out in the cold.[1]

BETWEEN YOU AND GOD

Take a mental inventory of your supplies for your life journey. What is useless baggage?

_____

_____

_____

What have you included from God's packing checklist:

❑ *love*   ❑ *joy*   ❑ *peace*   ❑ *patience*   ❑ *kindness*   ❑ *goodness*   ❑ *faithfulness*
❑ *gentleness*   ❑ *self-control*

_____

What would you like to say to the Lord?

_____

_____

_____

_____

_____

_____

_____

_____

_____

_____

_____

_____

_____

_____

_____

_____

_____

_____

_____

_____

_____

[1] Adapted from *A Gentle Thunder,* pp. 175-179.

Notes – Week Four

MEN RAISING THE STANDARD

*Love the LORD your God with all your heart
and with all your soul and with all your strength.*

Deuteronomy 6:5

RETREAT DISCUSSION GUIDE

Opening Discussion:

Do you think a first-time visitor to America would recognize us as a nation founded on God? Why or why not?

_____

_____

_____

_____

_____

KEY CONCEPT:

Men of God must be conformed to the image of God, rather than conformed to the image of men.

Introduction

Until you solidify your foundation, you will be wasting time and money fixing the cracks on your walls.

We have to take seriously what God expects of us.

We have too many people telling us how to be a man. We become men conformed to men, rather than men conformed to the image of God.

The Apostle Paul was not easily intimidated.

PHILIPPIANS 1:21
For to me, to live is Christ and to die is gain.

2 CORINTHIANS 4:17
For our light and momentary troubles are achieving for us an eternal glory that far outweighs them all.

Paul's attitude? "It doesn't matter to me. It's all Christ."

A messed-up man results ultimately in a messed-up planet!

Attributes of a Godly Man

1. _____ to his wife and family.

The essence of manhood is not how many women you can have, but how good you are at being faithful to one for a lifetime.

_____

_____

_____

_____

2. **Able to make and live out _____ choices.**

A part of what it means to be a man of God is going through the tough times and being faithful to God until He opens the door and brings you in your blessing.

_____

_____

_____

_____

3. **Sets the _____ for the world around him.**

Our sons are not the lost generation, but the product of a lost generation.

_____

_____

_____

_____

4. **Has an _____ perspective.**

Our lives have eternal value. It is not about what we leave behind, but what we forward ahead.

_____

_____

_____

_____

Stand up, O man of God. It's time to go public!

5. **Takes a stand for _____.**

   We should stop apologizing for living for Jesus Christ. Nobody else is apologizing. We ought to stand up and be the men God calls us to be.

   _____

   _____

   _____

   _____

6. **Understands that his faith is a _____ walk.**

   In church on Sunday is not where you learn to play the game. It is only like a huddle before the game.

   _____

   _____

   _____

   _____

7. **Able to do wonderful things when the _____ is against him.**

   _____

   _____

   _____

   _____

PSALM 27:3

Though an army besiege me, my heart will not fear;
   though war break out against me, even then will I be confident.

8. **Committed to _____.**

   You don't have to like it, you just have to obey.

   _____

   _____

   _____

   _____

"Unless God is telling you who you are, you don't know who you are."

"We have placed our manhood on the altar of money, personal peace, and affluence, rather than becoming men of character, men of integrity, and men of purity. We have sacrificed our manhood and Satan has slipped in and created a whole generation of boys who don't know how to be men."

9. Understands we are in a _____.

We are in a war for our children, for our families, and for our culture.

_____

_____

_____

_____

10. Seeks God for the _____ to fight every day.

Every day we have to fight. We need the power of God for that day.

_____

_____

_____

_____

The eyes of the Lord go to and fro looking for a man He can use.

11. Takes seriously the _____ of God.

We need to commit ourselves to God's standard—all of it.

_____

_____

_____

_____

12. Gets _____ _____ when he gets knocked down.

If you've already blown it, Good news! God can turn it around!

_____

_____

_____

_____

Group Discussion
(In pre-arranged groups of 3-4 men each)

What would you say is your strongest trait as a man of God?

_____
_____
_____
_____

Your weakest? (Please make note only of your own personal struggle.)

_____
_____
_____
_____
_____
_____
_____
_____
_____

Pray together for God's grace to live each day more fully for Christ.

God can take you from where you are and give you a brand-new start.

Notes

MEN OF GOD'S WORD

How can a young man keep his way pure?
By living according to your word.
I seek you with all my heart;
do not let me stray from your commands.
I have hidden your word in my heart
that I might not sin against you.

Psalm 119:9-11

RETREAT DISCUSSION GUIDE

MEN OF GOD'S WORD
JOSEPH STOWELL

Opening Reflection:

Suppose one of your children had a behavior problem. You and your wife do not agree on a solution. Where or from whom would you seek advice?

For single men:
Suppose you and a co-worker have difficulty getting along. Where or from whom would you seek advice?

_____

_____

_____

_____

_____

_____

KEY CONCEPT:

God's Word is the absolute standard and authority for every area of our lives.

Introduction

PSALM 1:1-3
*Blessed is the man
   who does not walk in the counsel of the wicked
or stand in the way of sinners
   or sit in the seat of mockers.
But his delight is in the law of the LORD,
   and on his law he meditates day and night.
He is like a tree planted by streams of water,
   which yields its fruit in season
 and whose leaf does not wither.
   Whatever he does prospers.*

Roy Regal's run for the goal was a matter of instinct. To him it seemed right. It seemed good. It was his moment of glory. It was *instinct* that drove him—and drove him the wrong way.

If we are not careful, we will be men whose whole lives are driven by our _____.

God calls us to be men shaped, molded, formed by the inspired

_____ _____ _____.

The Authority of Scripture

2 Timothy 3:16-17

All Scripture is inspired by God and profitable for teaching, for reproof, for correction, for training in righteousness; that the man of God may be adequate, equipped for every good work. (NASB)

The Bible is profitable for:

1. _____.
2. _____.
3. _____.
4. _____ _____ _____.

All Scripture is inspired by God. The literal translation for inspired is _____ - _____.

As we encounter the Word of God, we encounter God—God's wisdom, God's love for us, God's justice, God's righteousness.

_____

_____

There is not one _____ in this _____ that is not submissive to the authority of the Word of God.

_____

_____

_____

_____

"...I am the keeper of the lighthouse. Adjust three degrees!"

God's Word is clearly, finally, always true. It is the absolute standard and authority. God does not adjust to us; He is what is correct. We adjust to _____.

"The Bible is really like God in my hand—holding Him, hearing Him, reading Him. It is power, wisdom, correctness, justice, fairness, and love."

Light in the Darkness

The world says:	**The Bible says:**
Grab for _____, position and credentials	*Not so with you. Instead, whoever wants to become great among you must be your servant.* **(Mt. 20:26)**
We work to please our _____, get more pay, get promoted.	*Whatever you do, work at it with all your heart, as working for the Lord, not for men.* **(Col. 3:23)**
A man's _____ exists to make his life easier.	*Husbands, love your wives, just as Christ loved the church and gave himself up for her.* **(Ephes. 5:25)**
Money exists so we can accumulate _____ for our own benefit and significance.	*Command those who are rich in this present age not to be haughty, nor to trust in uncertain riches but in the living God, who gives us richly all things to enjoy. Let them do good, that they be rich in good works, ready to give, willing to share.* **(1 Tim. 6:17-18)**
We should be loaded with guilt and feel like abject _____ because of our mistakes.	*If we confess our sins, He is faithful and just to forgive us our sins and to cleanse us from all unrighteousness.* **(1 John 1:9)** *Come to me, all you who are weary and burdened, and I will give you rest. Take my yoke upon you and learn from me, for I am gentle and humble in heart, and you will find rest for your souls.* **(Mt.11:28-29)**

Matthew 5:23-24

Therefore if you bring your gift to the altar, and there remember that your brother has something against you, leave your gift there before the altar, and go your way. First be reconciled to your brother, and then come and offer your gift.

God's Word will not only train you, it will reprove your sin.

"Know this: If you become a man of God, He will chase you down with His Word. If you start running the wrong way, His Word is going to start screaming at you...Thank God it does! I do not want at the end of my life to be known as 'Wrong-Way Stowell.'"

> "I know what I need to do when I get done talking to my wife. I need to go out and wrestle with my kids on the floor because if God walked through that door, He would go wrestle with my kids... That's the kind of Father He is."

God Is a "Family Man"

EPHESIANS 6:4

And you, fathers, do not provoke your children to wrath, but bring them up in the training and admonition of the Lord.

What is the first thing you do at the end of the day when you come home to your family?

_____

_____

Is there need for some adjustment?

❑ Yes   ❑ No   ❑ Maybe

If so, what approach would be more-like-Jesus?

_____

_____

_____

_____

Ready for the Privilege of Good Works

Put down your pen for the next few minutes as you listen to Dr. Stowell's final illustration. Then answer the following questions before the discussion groups.

Why would Jesus take the seat next to the mentally-challenged young woman? Would you find it difficult to do the same?

_____

_____

_____

What changed Dr. Stowell's attitude?

_____

_____

_____

What was the unexpected reward for his obedience?

_____

_____

_____

Group Discussion
(In pre-arranged groups of 3-4 men each)

Look back at your answer to the reflection question posed at the beginning of this session regarding where you go for advice (page 67). Would your answer now differ from your original answer? Why, or why not?

_____

_____

_____

_____

What area of your life do you feel is governed more by instinct than the Word of God? Share briefly. (Please make note only of your own struggle. Do not write down another brother's sharing.)

_____

_____

_____

_____

_____

_____

_____

_____

_____

_____

Pray together for God's grace in the areas of struggle mentioned by each member of the group.

Like the Hound of Heaven, God's Word pounced on me again. "Stowell, I thought you were a man of the Word! Doesn't the Word of God say you should imitate Christ? Well, what do you think Jesus would do if He got on this plane?"

Notes

MEN WALKING WITH GOD

*Only be careful, and watch yourselves closely
so that you do not forget the things your eyes have seen
or let them slip from your heart as long as you live.
Teach them to your children and to their children after them.*

Deuteronomy 4:9

RETREAT DISCUSSION GUIDE

Opening Reflection:

Take a few moments in prayer. Write in the space below something that you would like the Lord to do in your heart this weekend.

_____

_____

_____

_____

_____

_____

KEY CONCEPT:

God is calling us to make ourselves totally available to him.

Introduction

The problems in our culture will not be solved by a sociological exposition of "the problem." They will not be solved by relationship alone. It's going to take the power of the Holy Ghost washing over our hearts, over our minds, and over our lives. To shed all of this "stuff" we are carrying and to lay it at the foot of the cross, we need a real gully-washing of the Spirit—*and a genuine brokenness.*

Something inside me said, "Crawford, go shake his hand." And I audibly said, "Not in this life."

What God is teaching us in Promise Keepers is all about doing what is right in the context of human history. It's not about how you're treated. It's not about what people do for you. But the real test of transformation is a decision in your soul to do the right thing for the right reason.

Isaiah Encounters God

Isaiah 6:1-8

In the year that King Uzziah died, I saw the Lord seated on a throne, high and exalted, and the train of his robe filled the temple. Above him were seraphs, each with six wings: With two wings they covered their faces, with two they covered their feet, and with two they were flying. And they were calling to one another:

"Holy, holy, holy is the LORD Almighty;
the whole earth is full of his glory."

At the sound of their voices the doorposts and thresholds shook and the temple was filled with smoke.

"Woe to me!" I cried. "I am ruined! For I am a man of unclean lips, and I live among a people of unclean lips, and my eyes have seen the King, the LORD Almighty."

Then one of the seraphs flew to me with a live coal in his hand, which he had taken with tongs from the altar. With it he touched my mouth and said, "See, this has touched your lips; your guilt is taken away and your sin atoned for."

Then I heard the voice of the Lord saying, "Whom shall I send? And who will go for us?"

And I said, "Here am I. Send me!"

Isaiah's experience forever changed his life, because he embraced the principles of intimacy with God.

1.   **Bask in God's** _____.

   _____

   _____

   _____

   _____

   _____

   _____

   _____

   _____

Once you have been into the inner sanctuary, you begin to plumb its depth and cultivate the power of your walking relationship with God.

"There must be a decision in your soul that no matter what circumstance you find yourself in, you will represent the King's business In this world."

The path to intimacy with God requires great brokenness.

2.   **Confront your own** _____.

_____
_____
_____
_____
_____
_____
_____
_____

Some of you may still be wrestling with strongholds in your life that are displeasing to God. And you've been hiding out. People may think that you're godly. You can dazzle them with your evangelical, theological articulation and smoke and mirrors. But you know in your heart of hearts that there is a compartment in your life that is tearing you up. And you have not heard the voice of God in so long that there is a drought in your soul.

3.   _____ **God's transforming work.**

_____
_____
_____
_____
_____
_____
_____
_____

"Information is not transformation. Content is not power. Exposure is not experience. What we need more than ever before in our history is brokenness."

> "Isaiah said, 'I saw the Lord!' The spiritual glaucoma had been taken away. The distraction of Uzziah and all of his greatness had been put to death. And Isaiah saw God as never before."

If You can use me, Lord, You know my frailties. I've seen You. There is none like You. I have nothing to bring to the table.

4.   **Submit and surrender your** _____.

_____
_____
_____
_____
_____
_____
_____

True greatness is not recognition or popularity. Greatness is godliness. Greatness is obedience. Greatness is faithfulness.

I am willing to go anywhere, to do anything, and to be anything that God wants me to be.

_____
_____
_____
_____
_____
_____
_____

Group Discussion

(Continue the same groups of 3-4 men each throughout the weekend.)

What are the distractions or strongholds in your life that keep you from hearing God clearly?

_____
_____
_____
_____
_____
_____
_____

What are your God-given responsibilities that need renewed zeal and direction?

_____
_____
_____
_____
_____
_____
_____
_____
_____
_____

Pray together for God's cleansing and a renewed desire for Him and the things of His Kingdom.

"Isaiah said, 'Then I heard the voice of the Lord....'

"The problem was not in God's ability to communicate. God was not silent; Isaiah was distracted. But after he had received cleansing, his ears were unstopped. He could hear God clearly."

Notes

MEN OF WORSHIP AND PRAYER

Because your love is better than life,
my lips will glorify you.
I will praise you as long as I live,
and in your name I will lift up my hands.

Psalm 63:3-4

RETREAT DISCUSSION GUIDE

Opening Reflection:

Do you enjoy worship or merely endure it? Why?

_____

_____

_____

_____

KEY CONCEPT:

Worship is a transforming encounter with God which reveals who we are and what we are made for.

Exodus 3:1-12

Now Moses was tending the flock of Jethro his father-in-law, the priest of Midian, and he led the flock to the far side of the desert and came to Horeb, the mountain of God. There the angel of the LORD appeared to him in flames of fire from within a bush. Moses saw that though the bush was on fire it did not burn up. So Moses thought, "I will go over and see this strange sight—why the bush does not burn up."

When the LORD saw that he had gone over to look, God called to him from within the bush, "Moses! Moses!"

And Moses said, "Here I am."

"Do not come any closer," God said. "Take off your sandals, for the place where you are standing is holy ground." Then he said, "I am the God of your father, the God of Abraham, the God of Isaac and the God of Jacob." At this, Moses hid his face, because he was afraid to look at God.

The LORD said, "I have indeed seen the misery of my people in Egypt. I have heard them crying out because of their slave drivers, and I am concerned about their suffering. So I have come down to rescue them from the hand of the Egyptians and to bring them up out of that land into a good and spacious land, a land flowing with milk and honey–the home of the Canaanites, Hittites, Amorites, Perizzites, Hivites and Jebusites. And now the cry of the Israelites has reached me, and I have seen the way the Egyptians are oppressing them. So now, go. I am sending you to Pharaoh to bring my people the Israelites out of Egypt."

But Moses said to God, "Who am I, that I should go to Pharaoh and bring the Israelites out of Egypt?"

And God said, "I will be with you. And this will be the sign to you that it is I who have sent you: When you have brought the people out of Egypt, you will worship God on this mountain."

Worship Action Points:

1. Turn _____

2. _____ up

3. _____ down

4. Be _____

"A man's walk with God only becomes effective when he learns to worship and to live a life of prayer."

Moses Meets His Creator

Three things Moses found as he encountered God on the mountain:

1. **The** _____ **of God**: *Confidence*
    You will find out who you are in the presence of the One who shows you who He is.
    God knew where Moses was, his mistakes of the past.
    God knew Moses' name and had affection for him.

    _____

    _____

    _____

    _____

    ISAIAH 49:16 *See, I have engraved you on the palms of my hands.*
    Jesus knows your name. We are on his mind.

    God knew Moses' heart.
    When God sees a man who has turned aside for him, he will meet him in a transforming encounter.

    _____

    _____

    _____

    _____

2. **The** _____ **of God**: *Purpose*
    Moses [and we] will worship God ongoingly.
    We are transformed and become instruments of liberation for others.

    _____

    _____

    _____

    _____

3. **A** _____ **with God**: *Direction*
    Take your shoes off, for this is holy ground.

    _____

    _____

    _____

    _____

Take Off Your Shoes

1. **The _____ of Moses' own hands**. We all essentially have made our shoes.
   - ➢ Step out of what you have made with your own hands and step onto what I have fashioned with mine.
   - ➢ Out of your resources and into mine.
   - ➢ Move out of dependence on your own resources and proving yourself, to dependency on God.
   - ➢ Holy ground was bought by the blood of Jesus at the cross.

   _____

   _____

   _____

The soles of shoes have "stuff" on them.

2. **The stains, the shame of the _____**. The soles of the shoes have "stuff" stuck to them. Stuff gets stuck to *your* soul. You have walked in sin; corruption stinks.
   - ➢ He will cleanse us on holy ground.
   - ➢ He calls us to a daily walk, a daily cleansing.

   _____

   _____

   _____

Bare feet bring about a whole new walk.

3. **The pace of his own _____**. One walks a lot slower and more carefully without shoes. It is the slowness of waiting before God.

   _____

   _____

   _____

   _____

This encounter with God launched Moses in a lifetime of effective leadership to his people. We, too are launched into a ministry of _____ for our families.

"God gives worship to us not so much as a mandate, but more as a gift."

Entering God's Presence

"We are not called to an experience of just a week-end with God. We are called to a journey for the rest of our life, to chart a pathway to walk forward in the call of God."

A daily pattern:

1. Turn aside

_____
_____
_____
_____

2. Listen up

_____
_____
_____
_____

3. Strip down

_____
_____
_____
_____

4. Be filled

_____
_____
_____
_____

Open hands

> Signify a person _____ to God;

_____
_____
_____

> Surrendering things we have _____ with our hands, things we would rather not talk about;

_____
_____

➢ Offer our hands for His _____

_____

_____

_____

Briefly stop the video after Pastor Jack's instructions for sharing. Resume the
video after men at the retreat finish praying for one another.

Share Your Hearts
(In small groups)

What is ground into your soul that needs to be removed and
cleansed by God before you can be an instrument of liberation
for your family and the family of God?

_____

_____

_____

_____

Pray for each other's expressed needs.

No matter how ineptly, how imperfectly, how inadequately, or how tragically your life has worked in trying to fulfill God's will, the Lord's heart for you has not changed. God will *never* give up on you.

Notes

FACE TO FACE
An Encounter with Christ

Dropping Your Rocks
Forgive and Accept

YOUR SACK OF STONES

MATTHEW 11:28-29
"Come to me, all of you who are tired and have heavy loads, and I will give you rest. Accept my teachings and learn from me, because I am gentle and humble in spirit, and you will find rest for your lives. The teaching I ask you to accept is easy; the load I give you to carry is light" (NCV).

Y ou have one. A sack. A burlap sack. Probably aren't aware of it, may not have been told about it. Could be you don't remember it. But it was given to you. A sack. An itchy, scratchy burlap sack.

You needed the sack so you could carry the stones. Rocks, boulders, pebbles. All sizes. All shapes. All unwanted.

You didn't request them. You didn't seek them. But you were given them.

Don't remember?

Some were rocks of rejection. You were given one the time you didn't pass the tryout. It wasn't for lack of effort. Heaven only knows how much you practiced. You thought you were good enough for the team. But the coach didn't. The instructor didn't. You thought you were good enough, but they said you weren't.

They and how many others?

You don't have to live long before you get a collection of stones. Make a poor grade. Make a bad choice. Make a mess. Get called a few names. Get mocked. Get abused.

And the stones don't stop with adolescence. I sent a letter this week to an unemployed man who's been rejected in more than fifty interviews.

And so the sack gets heavy. Heavy with stones. Stones of rejection. Stones we don't deserve.

Along with a few we do.

Look into the burlap sack and you see that not all the stones are from rejections. There is a second type of stone. The stone of regret.

Regret for the time you lost your temper.

Regret for the day you lost control.

Regret for the moment you lost your pride.

Regret for the years you lost your priorities.

And even regret for the hour you lost your innocence.

One stone after another, one guilty stone after another.

With time the sack gets heavy. We get tired. How can you have dreams for the future when all your energy is required to shoulder the past?

No wonder some people look miserable. The sack slows the step. The sack chafes. Helps explain the irritation on so many faces, the sag in so many steps, the drag in so many shoulders, and most of all, the desperation in so many acts.

You're consumed with doing whatever it takes to get some rest.

So you take the sack to the office. You resolve to work so hard you'll forget about the sack. You arrive early and stay late. People are impressed. But when it's time to go home, there is the sack–waiting to be carried out.

You carry the stones into happy hour. With a name like that, it must bring relief. So you set the sack on the floor, sit on the stool, and drink a few. The music gets loud, and your head gets light. But then it's time to go. You look down, and there is the sack.

You drag it into therapy. You sit on the couch with the sack at your feet and spill all your stones on the floor and name them one by one. The therapist listens. She empathizes. Some helpful counsel is given. But when the time is up, you're obliged to gather the rocks and take them with you.

Some even take the sack to church. Perhaps religion will help, you reason. But instead of removing a few stones, some well-meaning but misguided preacher may add to the load. God's messengers sometimes give more hurt than help. And you might leave the church with a few new rocks in your sack.

The result? A person slugging his way through life, weighed down by the past. I don't know if you've noticed, but it's hard to be thoughtful when you're carrying a burlap sack. It's hard to be affirming when you are affirmation starved. It's hard to be forgiving when you feel guilty.

Paul had an interesting observation about the way we treat people. He said it about marriage, but the principle applies in any relationship. "[The man] who loves his wife loves himself" (Eph. 5:28 NCV). There is a correlation between the way you feel about yourself and the way you feel about others. If you are at peace with yourself–if you like yourself–you will get along with others.

The converse is also true. If you don't like yourself, if you are ashamed, embarrassed, or angry, other people are going to know it. The tragic part of the burlap-sack story is we tend to throw our stones at those we love.

Unless the cycle is interrupted.

Which takes us to the question, "How *does* a person get relief?"

Which, in turn, takes us to one of the kindest verses in the Bible, "Come to me, all of you who are tired and have heavy loads, and I will give you rest. Accept my teachings and learn from me, because I am gentle and humble in spirit, and you will find rest for your lives. The teaching I ask you to accept is easy; the load I give you to carry is light" (Mt. II:28-29 NCV).

You knew I was going to say that. I can see you holding this book and shaking your head. "I've tried that. I've read the Bible, I've sat on the pew–but I've never received relief."

If that is the case, could I ask a delicate but deliberate question? Could it be that you went to religion and didn't go to God? Could it be that you went to a church but never saw Christ?

"Come to me," the verse reads.

It's easy to go to the wrong place. Jesus says he is the solution for weariness of soul.

Go to him. Be honest with him. Admit you have soul secrets you've never dealt with. He already knows what they are. He's just waiting for you to ask him to help. He's just waiting for you to give him your sack.

Go ahead. You'll be glad you did. (Those near to you will be glad as well . . . it's hard to throw stones when you've left your sack at the cross.)[1]

BETWEEN YOU AND GOD

Name some stones in your sack.

_____

_____

_____

What would you like to say to the Lord?

_____

_____

_____

_____

_____

_____

_____

_____

_____

_____

---

[1] *When God Whispers Your Name*, pp.111-115.

THE HEAVINESS OF HATRED

EPHESIANS 4:32
Be kind and loving to each other, and forgive each other, just as God forgave you in Christ. (NCV)

Each week Kevin Tunell is required to mail a dollar to a family he'd rather forget. They sued him for $1.5 million but settled for $936, to be paid a dollar at a time. The family expects the payment each Friday so Tunell won't forget what happened on the first Friday of 1982. That's the day their daughter was killed.

Tunell was convicted of manslaughter and drunken driving. He was seventeen. She was eighteen. Tunell served a court sentence. He also spent seven years campaigning against drunk driving, six years more than his sentence required. But he keeps forgetting to send the dollar.

The weekly restitution is to last until the year 2000. Eighteen years. Tunell makes the check out to the victim, mails it to her family, and the money is deposited in a scholarship fund.

The family has taken him to court four times for failure to comply. After the most recent appearance, Tunell spent thirty days in jail. He insists that he's not defying the order but rather is haunted by the girl's death and tormented by the reminders. He offered the family two boxes of checks covering the payments until the year 2001, one year more than required. They refused. It's not money they seek, but penance.

Few would question the anger of the family. Only the naive would think it fair to leave the guilty unpunished. But I do have one concern. Is 936 payments enough? Not for Tunell to send, mind you, but for the family to demand? When they receive the final payment, will they be at peace? In August 2000, will the family be able to put the matter to rest? Is eighteen years' worth of restitution sufficient? Will 196 months' worth of remorse be adequate?

How much is enough? Were you in the family and were Tunell your target, how many payments would you require? Better stated, how many payments do you require?

No one—I repeat, no one—makes it through life free of injury. Someone somewhere has hurt you. Like the eighteen-year-old, you've been a victim. She died because someone drank too much. Part of you has died because someone spoke too much, demanded too much, or neglected too much.

Everyone gets wounded; hence everyone must decide: how many payments will I demand? We may not require that the offender write checks, but we have other ways of settling the score.

Silence is a popular technique. (Ignore them when they speak.) Distance is equally effective. (When they come your way, walk the other.) Nagging is a third tool for revenge. ("Oh, I see you still have fingers on your hand. Funny you never use them to dial my number." "Oh, Joe, nice of you to drop in on us unpromoted peons.")

Amazing how creative we can be at getting even. If I can soil one evening, spoil one day, foil one Friday, then justice is served and I'm content.

For now. Until I think of you again. Until I see you again. Until something happens that brings to mind the deed you did, then I'll demand another check. I'm not about to let you heal before I do. As long as I suffer, you suffer. As long as I hurt, you hurt. You cut me, and I'm going to make you feel bad as long as I bleed, even if I have to reopen the wound myself.

Call it a bad addiction. We start the habit innocently enough, indulging our hurts with doses of anger. Not much, just a needle or two of rancor. The rush numbs the hurt, so we come back for more and up the dosage; we despise not only what he did, but who he is. Insult him. Shame him. Ridicule him. The surge energizes. Drugged on malice, the roles are reversed; we aren't the victim, we're the victor. It feels good. Soon we hate him and anyone like him. ("All men are jerks." "Every preacher is a huckster." "You can't trust a woman.") The progression is predictable. Hurt becomes hate, and hate becomes rage as we become junkies unable to make it through the day without mainlining on bigotry and bitterness.

Your friend broke his promises? Your boss didn't keep her word? I'm sorry, but before you take action, answer this question: How did God react when you broke your promises to him?

You've been lied to? It hurts to be deceived. But before you double your fists, think: How did God respond when you lied to him?

You've been neglected? Forgotten? Left behind? Rejection hurts. But before you get even, get honest with yourself. Have you ever neglected God? Have you always been attentive to his will? None of us have. How did he react when you neglected him?

The key to forgiving others is to quit focusing on what they did to you and start focusing on what God did for you.

But, Max, that's not fair! Somebody has to pay for what he did.

I agree. Someone must pay, and Someone already has.

You don't understand, Max, this guy doesn't deserve grace. He doesn't deserve mercy. He's not worthy of forgiveness.

I'm not saying he is. But are you?

Besides, what other choice do you have? Hatred? The alternative is not appealing. Unforgiving servants always end up in prison. Prisons of anger, guilt, and depression. God doesn't have to put us in a jail; we create our own.

Let me be very clear. Hatred will sour your outlook and break your back. The load of bitterness is simply too heavy. Your knees will buckle under the strain, and your heart will break beneath the weight. The mountain before you is steep enough without the heaviness of hatred on your back. The wisest choice–the only choice–is for you to drop the anger. You will never be called upon to give anyone more grace than God has already given you.[1]

BETWEEN YOU AND GOD

List below some people whom you avoid or punish because of your anger toward them. Note also their offense.

Person	Offense	Person	Offense
_____	_____	_____	_____
_____	_____	_____	_____
_____	_____	_____	_____

Note the date when you are ready to release them: _____
(Date)

What would you like to say to the Lord?

_____
_____
_____
_____
_____
_____
_____
_____
_____
_____
_____
_____
_____
_____
_____

---

[1] Adapted from *In the Grip of Grace,* pp. 149-157.

READ THE STORY

LUKE 24:13-16

That same day two of Jesus' followers were going to a town named Emmaus, about seven miles from Jerusalem. They were talking about everything that had happened. While they were talking and discussing, Jesus himself came near and began walking with them, but they were kept from recognizing him. (NCV)

Their world has tumbled in on them. It's obvious by the way they walk. Their feet shuffle, their heads hang, their shoulders droop. The seven miles from Jerusalem to Emmaus must feel like seventy.

As they walk they talk "about everything that had happened" (Lk. 24:14 NCV). It's not hard to imagine their words.

"Why did the people turn against him?"

"He could have come down from the cross. Why didn't he?"

"He just let Pilate push him around."

"What do we do now?"

As they walk, a stranger comes up behind them. It is Jesus, but they don't recognize him. Disappointment will do that to you. It will blind you to the very presence of God. Discouragement turns our eyes inward. God could be walking next to us, but despair clouds our vision.

Despair does something else. Not only does it cloud our vision, it hardens our hearts. We get cynical. We get calloused. And when good news comes, we don't want to accept it for fear of being disappointed again. That's what happened to these two people.

The disciples had hoped Jesus would free Israel. They had hoped he'd kick out the Romans. They'd hoped Pilate would be out and Jesus would be in. But Pilate was still in, and Jesus was dead.

Unfulfilled expectations. God didn't do what they wanted him to.

They knew what they expected of Jesus. They knew what he was supposed to do. They didn't have to ask him. If Jesus is the Messiah, he won't sleep in my storm. He won't ever die. He won't defy tradition. He'll do what he is supposed to do.

But that's not what he did. And aren't we glad? Aren't we glad the prayer of Cleopas and his friend went unanswered? Aren't we glad God didn't adjust his agenda to fulfill the requests of these two disciples?

They were good disciples. With good hearts. And sincere prayers. They just had the wrong expectations.

When my oldest daughter was about six years old, she and I were having a discussion about my work. It seems she wasn't too happy with my chosen profession. She wanted me to leave the ministry. "I like you as a preacher," she explained. "I just really wish you sold snow cones."

An honest request from a pure heart. It made sense to her that the happiest people in the world were the men who drove the snow-cone trucks. You play music. You sell goodies. You make kids happy. What more could you want? (Come to think about it, she may have a point. I could get a loan, buy a truck and . . . Naw, I'd eat too much.)

I heard her request, but I didn't heed it. Why? Because I knew better. I know what I'm called to do and what I need to do. The fact is I know more about life than she does.

And the point is, God knows more about life than we do.

People wanted him to redeem Israel, but he knew better. He would rather his people be temporarily oppressed than eternally lost. When forced to choose between battling Pilate and battling Satan, he chose the battle we couldn't win. He said no to what they wanted and yes to what they needed. He said no to a liberated Israel and yes to a liberated humanity.

And once again, aren't we glad he did? And aren't we glad he does?

Now be honest. Are we glad he says no to what we want and yes to what we need? Not always. If we ask for a new marriage, and he says honor the one you've got, we aren't happy. If we ask for healing, and he says learn through the pain, we aren't happy. If we ask for more money, and he says treasure the unseen, we aren't always happy.

When God doesn't do what we want, it's not easy. Never has been. Never will be. But faith is the conviction that God knows more than we do about this life and he will get us through it.

Remember, disappointment is caused by unmet expectations.

Disappointment is cured by revamped expectations.

I like that story about the fellow who went to the pet store in search of a singing parakeet. Seems he was a bachelor and his house was too quiet. The store owner had just the bird for him, so the man bought it. The next day the bachelor came home from work to a house full of music. He went to the cage to feed the bird and noticed for the first time that the parakeet had only one leg.

He felt cheated that he'd been sold a one-legged bird, so he called and complained.

"What do you want," the store owner responded, "a bird who can sing or a bird who can dance?"

Good question for times of disappointment. What do we want? That's what Jesus asks the disciples. What do you want? Do you want temporary freedom–or eternal freedom? Jesus sets about the task of restructuring their expectations.

You know what he did? He told them the story. Not just any story. He told them the story of God and God's plan for people. "Then starting with what Moses and all the prophets had said about him, Jesus began to explain everything that had been written about himself in the Scriptures" (v. 27).

Fascinating. Jesus' cure for the broken heart is the story of God. He started with Moses and finished with himself. Why did he do that? Why did he retell the ancient tale? Why did he go all the way back two thousand years to the story of Moses? I think I know the reason. I know because what they heard is what we all need to hear when we are disappointed.

We need to hear that God is still in control. We need to hear that it's not over until he says so. We need to hear that life's mishaps and tragedies are not a reason to bail out. They are simply a reason to sit tight.

The way to deal with discouragement? The cure for disappointment? Go back to the story. Read it again and again. Be reminded that you aren't the first person to weep. And you aren't the first person to be helped.

Read the story and remember, their story is yours!

The challenge too great? Read the story. That's you crossing the Red Sea with Moses.

Too many worries? Read the story. That's you receiving heavenly food with the Israelites.

Your wounds too deep? Read the story. That's you, Joseph, forgiving your brothers for betraying you.

Your enemies too mighty? Read the story. That's you marching with Jehoshaphat into a battle already won.

Your disappointments too heavy? Read the story of the Emmaus-bound disciples. The Savior they thought was dead now walked beside them. He entered their house and sat at their table. And something happened in their hearts. "It felt like a fire burning in us when Jesus talked to us on the road and explained the Scriptures to us" (Lk. 24:31 NCV).

Next time you're disappointed, don't panic. Don't jump out. Don't give up. Just be patient and let God remind you he's still in control. It ain't over till it's over.[1]

BETWEEN YOU AND GOD

Do you search God's Word for answers to your problems?

_____

_____

What would you like to say to the Lord?

_____

_____

_____

_____

_____

---

[1] Adapted from *He Still Moves Stones,* pp. 76-81.

THE FATHER IN THE FACE OF THE ENEMY

MATTHEW 5:7-9
Blessed are the merciful, for they will be shown mercy.
Blessed are the pure in heart, for they will see God.
Blessed are the peacemakers, for they will be called sons of God.

Daniel is big. He used to make his living by lifting weights and teaching others to do the same. His scrapbook is colorful with ribbons and photos of him in his prime, striking the muscle-man pose and flexing the bulging arms.

The only thing bigger than Daniel's biceps is his heart. Let me tell you about a time his heart became tender.

Daniel was living in the city of Porto Alegre, Brazil. He worked at a gym and dreamed of owning his own. The bank agreed to finance the purchase if he could find someone to cosign the note. His brother agreed.

They filled out all the applications and awaited the approval. Everything went smoothly, and Daniel soon received a call from the bank telling him he could come and pick up the check. As soon as he got off work, he went to the bank.

When the loan officer saw Daniel, he looked surprised and asked Daniel why he had come.

"To pick up the check," Daniel explained.

"That's funny," responded the banker. "Your brother was in here earlier. He picked up the money and used it to retire the mortgage on his house."

Daniel was incensed. He never dreamed his own brother would trick him like that. He stormed over to his brother's house and pounded on the door. The brother answered the door with his daughter in his arms. He knew Daniel wouldn't hit him if he was holding a child.

He was right. Daniel didn't hit him. But he promised his brother that if he ever saw him again he would break his neck.

Daniel went home, his big heart bruised and ravaged by the trickery of his brother. He had no other choice but to go back to the gym and work to pay off the debt.

A few months later, Daniel met a young American missionary named Allen Dutton. Allen befriended Daniel and taught him about Jesus Christ. Daniel and his wife soon became Christians and devoted disciples.

But though Daniel had been forgiven so much, he still found it impossible to forgive his brother. The wound was deep. The pot of revenge still simmered. He didn't see his brother for two years. Daniel couldn't bring himself to look into the face of the one who had betrayed him. And his brother liked his own face too much to let Daniel see it.

But an encounter was inevitable. Both knew they would eventually run into each other. And neither knew what would happen then. The encounter occurred one day on a busy avenue. Let Daniel tell you in his own words what happened:

I saw him, but he didn't see me. I felt my fists clench and my face get hot. My initial impulse was to grab him around the throat and choke the life out of him.

But as I looked into his face, my anger began to melt. For as I saw him, I saw the image of my father. I saw my father's eyes. I saw my father's look. I saw my father's expression. And as I saw my father in his face, my enemy once again became my brother.

Daniel walked toward him. The brother stopped, turned, and started to run, but he was too slow. Daniel reached out and grabbed his shoulder. The brother winced, expecting the worst. But rather than have his throat squeezed by Daniel's hands, he found himself hugged by Daniel's big arms. And the two brothers stood in the middle of the river of people and wept.

Daniel's words are worth repeating: "When I saw the image of my father in his face, my enemy became my brother."

Seeing the father's image in the face of the enemy. Try that. The next time you see or think of the one who broke your heart, look twice. As you look at his face, look also for his face–the face of the One who forgave you. Look into the eyes of the King who wept when you pleaded for mercy. Look into the face of the Father who gave you grace when no one else gave you a chance. Find the face of the God who forgives in the face of your enemy. And then, set your enemy–and yourself–free.

And allow the hole in your heart to heal.[1]

BETWEEN YOU AND GOD

Suppose that tomorrow you were to run into someone who had wronged you deeply. What could you do to change your current view of this person and see the face of your Father?

_____

_____

_____

What would you like to say to the Lord?

_____

_____

_____

_____

_____

_____

_____

_____

_____

_____

_____

_____

_____

_____

_____

[1] *The Applause of Heaven,* pp. 116-119.

WHEN YOU AND YOUR KIN CAN'T

GALATIANS 4:7
So you are no longer a slave, but a son; and since you are a son, God has made you also an heir.

"Give me a word picture to describe a relative in your life who really bugs you."

I was asking the question of a half-dozen friends sitting around a lunch table. They all gave me one of those what-in-the-world? expressions. So I explained.

"I keep meeting people who can't deal with somebody in their family. Either their mother-in-law is a witch or their uncle is a bum or they have a father who treats them like they were never born."

Now their heads nodded. We were connecting. And the word pictures started coming.

"I've got a description," one volunteered. "A parasite on my neck. My wife has this brother who never works and always expects us to provide."

"A cactus wearing a silk shirt," said another. "It's my mother. She looks nice. Everyone thinks she's the greatest, but get close to her and she is prickly, dry, and . . . thirsty for life."

"A marble column," was the way another described an aunt. Dignified, noble, but high and hard.

"Tar baby in Br'er Rabbit," someone responded. Everyone understood the reference except me. I didn't remember the story of Br'er Rabbit. I asked for the short version. Wily Fox played a trick on Br'er Rabbit. The fox made a doll out of tar and stuck it on the side of the road. When Rabbit saw the tar baby, he thought it was a person and stopped to visit.

It was a one-sided conversation. The tar baby's silence bothered the rabbit. He couldn't stand to be next to someone and not communicate with them. So in his frustration he hit the tar baby and stuck to it. He hit the tar baby again with the other hand and, you guessed it, the other hand got stuck.

"That's how we are with difficult relatives," my fable-using friend explained. "We're stuck to someone we can't communicate with."

Stuck is right. It's not as if they are a neighbor you can move away from or an employee you can fire. They are family. And you can choose your friends, but you can't . . . well, you know.

Odds are, you probably know very well.

You've probably got a tar baby in your life, someone you can't talk to and can't walk away from. A mother who whines, an uncle who slurps his soup, or a sister who flaunts her figure. A dad who is still waiting for you to get a real job or a mother-in-law who wonders why her daughter married you.

Tar-baby relationships–stuck together but falling apart.

If we expect anyone to be sensitive to our needs, it is our family members. When we hurt physically, we want our family to respond. When we struggle emotionally, we want our family to know.

But sometimes they act like they don't know. Sometimes they act like they don't care. What can you do when those closest to you keep their distance? When you can get along with others, but you and your kin can't?

Does Jesus have anything to say about dealing with difficult relatives? Is there an example of Jesus bringing peace to a painful family? Yes, there is. His own.

It may surprise you to know that his family was less than perfect. They were. If your family doesn't appreciate you, take heart, neither did Jesus' family: "A prophet is honored everywhere except in his hometown and with his own people and in his own home" (Mark 6:4).

Each of us has a fantasy that our family will be like the Waltons, an expectation that our dearest friends will be our next of kin. Jesus didn't have that expectation. Look how he defined his family: "My true brother and sister and mother are those who do what God wants" (Mark 3:35 NCV).

When Jesus' brothers didn't share his convictions, he didn't try to force them. He recognized that his spiritual family could provide what his physical family didn't. If Jesus himself couldn't force his family to share his convictions, what makes you think you can force yours?

We can't control the way our family responds to us. When it comes to the behavior of others toward us, our hands are tied. We have to move beyond the naive expectation that if we do good, people will treat us right. The fact is they may and they may not—we cannot control how people respond to us.

If your father is a jerk, you could be the world's best son and he still won't tell you so.

If your aunt doesn't like your career, you could change jobs a dozen times and still never satisfy her.

If your sister is always complaining about what you got and she didn't, you could give her everything and she still may not change.

It's a game with unfair rules and fatal finishes. Jesus didn't play it, nor should you.

We don't know if Joseph affirmed his son Jesus in his ministry–but we know God did: "This is my Son, whom I love, and I am very pleased with him" (Mt. 3:17 NCV).

I can't assure you that your family will ever give you the blessing you seek, but I know God will. Let God give you what your family doesn't. If your earthly father doesn't affirm you, then let your heavenly Father take his place.

How do you do that? By emotionally accepting God as your father. You see, it's one thing to accept him as Lord, another to recognize him as Savior-but it's another matter entirely to accept him as Father.

To recognize God as Lord is to acknowledge that he is sovereign and supreme in the universe. To accept him as Savior is to accept his gift of salvation offered on the cross. To regard him as Father is to go a step further. Ideally, a father is the one in your life who provides and protects. That is exactly what God has done.

He has provided for your needs (Mt. 6:25-34). He has protected you from harm (Ps. 139:5). He has adopted you (Eph. 1:5). And he has given you his name (1 John 3:1).

God has proven himself as a faithful father. Now it falls to us to be trusting children. Let God give you what your family doesn't. Let him fill the void others have left. Rely upon him for your affirmation and encouragement. Having your family's approval is desirable but not necessary for happiness and not always possible. Jesus did not let the difficult dynamic of his family overshadow his call from God. And because he didn't, this message has a happy ending.

What happened to Jesus' family?

Mine with me a golden nugget hidden in a vein of the Book of Acts. "Then [the disciples] went back to Jerusalem from the Mount of Olives .... They all continued praying together with some women, *including Mary the mother of Jesus, and Jesus' brothers*" (Acts 1:12,14 NCV, emphasis added).

What a change! The ones who mocked him now worship him. The ones who pitied him now pray for him. What if Jesus had disowned them? Or worse still, what if he'd suffocated his family with his demand for change?

He didn't. He instead gave them space, time, and grace. And because he did, they changed. How much did they change? One brother became an apostle (Gal. 1:19) and others became missionaries (1 Cor. 9:5).

So don't lose heart. God still changes families. A tar baby today might be your dearest friend tomorrow.[1]

BETWEEN YOU AND GOD

Describe the perfect father. Does your heavenly Father fit your image? If not, could you be missing something he wants you to have?

_____

_____

What would you like to say to the Lord?

_____

_____

_____

_____

_____

---

[1] Adapted from *He Still Moves Stones,* pp. 29-35.

Notes – Week One

FACE TO FACE
An Encounter with Christ

POST-RETREAT DEVOTIONAL
WEEK TWO

Life on the Vine
Abide in Jesus

HIS SUMMIT

MATTHEW 5:1
Now when he saw the crowds, he went up on a mountainside and sat down.

If you have time to read this page, you probably don't need to.

If you are reading slowly in order to have something to occupy your time . . . if your reading hour is leisurely sandwiched between a long stroll and a good nap . . . if your list of things to do today was done an hour after you got up . . . then you might want to skip over to the next page. You probably have mastered this message.

If, however, you are reading in your car with one eye on the stoplight . . . or in the airport with one ear listening for your flight . . . or in bed late at night, knowing you have to get up early in the morning . . . then read on, friend. This is for you.

You are in a hurry. America is in a hurry. Time has sky-rocketed in value. The value of any commodity depends on its scarcity. And time that once was abundant now is going to the highest bidder.

A man in Florida bills his ophthalmologist ninety dollars for keeping him waiting one hour.

Twenty bucks will pay someone to pick up your cleaning.

Fifteen hundred bucks will buy a fax machine . . . for your car.

Greeting cards can be purchased to express to your children things you want to say, but don't have time to: "Have a great day at school" or "I wish I were there to tuck you in."

America–the country of shortcuts and fast lanes. (We're the only nation on earth with a mountain called "Rushmore.") Do we really have less time? Or is it just our imagination?

In 1965 a testimony before a Senate subcommittee claimed the future looked bright for free time in America. By 1985, predicted the report, Americans would be working twenty-two hours a week and would be able to retire at age thirty-eight. The reason? The computer age would usher in a gleaming array of advances that would do our work for us while stabilizing our economy.

And now, years later, . . . the computers are byting, the VCRs are recording, the fax machines are faxing. Yet the clocks are still ticking, and people are still running. The truth is, the average amount of leisure time has shrunk 37 percent since 1973. The average work week has increased from forty-one to forty-seven hours. (And, for many of you, forty-seven hours would be a calm week.)'

"I've got so many irons in the fire, I can't keep any of them hot," complained one young father.

Can you relate?

"When he saw the crowds, he went up on a mountainside . . . ."

Don't read the sentence so fast you miss the surprise. Matthew didn't write what you would expect him to. The verse doesn't read, "When he saw the crowds, he went into their midst." Or "When he saw the crowds, he healed their hurts." Or "When he saw the crowds, he seated them and began to teach them." On other occasions he did that . . . but not this time.

Before he went to the masses, he went to the mountain. Before the disciples encountered the crowds, they encountered the Christ. And before they faced the people, they were reminded of the sacred.

His summit. Clean air. Clear view. Crisp breeze. The roar of the marketplace is down there, and the perspective of the peak is up here.

Gently your guide invites you to sit on the rock above the tree line and look out with him at the ancient peaks that will never erode. "What is necessary is still what is sure," he confides. "Just remember:

"You'll go nowhere tomorrow that I haven't already been.

"Truth will still triumph.

"Death will still die.

"The victory is yours.

"And delight is one decision away–seize it."

The sacred summit. A place of permanence in a world of transition.

Think about the people in your world. Can't you tell the ones who have been to his mountain? Oh, their problems aren't any different. And their challenges are just as severe. But there is a stubborn peace that enshrines them. A confidence that life isn't toppled by unmet budgets or rerouted airplanes. A serenity that softens the corners of their lips. A contagious delight sparkling in their eyes.

And in their hearts reigns a fortresslike confidence that the valley can be endured, even enjoyed, because the mountain is only a decision away.

I read recently about a man who had breathed the summit air. His trips up the trail began early in his life and sustained him to the end. A few days before he died, a priest went to visit him in the hospital. As the priest entered the room, he noticed an empty chair beside the man's bed. The priest asked him if someone had been by to visit. The old man smiled, "I place Jesus on that chair, and I talk to him."

The priest was puzzled, so the man explained. "Years ago a friend told me that prayer was as simple as talking to a good friend. So every day I pull up a chair, invite Jesus to sit, and we have a good talk."

Some days later, the daughter of this man came to the parish house to inform the priest that her father had just died. "Because he seemed so content," she said, "I left him in his room alone for a couple of hours. When I got back to the room, I found him dead. I noticed a strange thing, though: His head was resting, not on the pillow, but on an empty chair that was beside his bed. "[1]

Learn a lesson from the man with the chair. Take a trip with the King to the mountain peak. It's pristine, uncrowded, and on top of the world. Stubborn joy begins by breathing deep up there before you go crazy down here.

Oops, I think I hear someone calling your flight ....[2]

BETWEEN YOU AND GOD

When Jesus invites you to join him on his summit, what is your most common response?

_____

_____

_____

What would you like to say to the Lord?

_____

_____

_____

_____

_____

_____

_____

_____

_____

_____

_____

_____

_____

_____

_____

---

[1] Walter Burkhardt, *Tell the Next Generation,* (Ramsey, NH: Paulist, 1982) p. 80.
[2] Adapted from *The Applause of Heaven,* pp. 17-24.

LATE-NIGHT GOOD NEWS

JOHN 16:33
I have told you these things, so that in me you may have peace. In this world you will have trouble. But take heart! I have overcome the world.

Late-night news is a poor sedative.
Last night it was for me. All I wanted was the allergen count and the basketball scores. But to get them, I had to endure the usual monologue of global misery. And last night the world seemed worse than usual.

Watching the news doesn't usually disturb me so. I'm not a gloom-and-doom sort of fellow. I feel I'm as good as the next guy in taking human tragedy with a spoon of faith. But last night . . . well, the world seemed dark.

Perhaps it was the two youngsters shot in a drive-by shooting–one was six, the other ten.

Perhaps it was the reassuring announcement that twenty-six thousand highway bridges in America are near collapse.

Our surgeon general, who is opposed to tobacco, wants to legalize drugs.

A billionaire rock star is accused of molesting children. One senator is accused of seducing associates, another of tampering with election procedures.

A rising political figure in Russia has earned the nickname of Hitler.

Pistol-packing drivers give rise to a new bumper sticker: "Keep honking. I'm reloading."

The national debt is deeper. Our taxes are higher, the pollen count is up, and the Dallas Mavericks lost their fifteenth game in a row.

"And that's the world tonight!" the well-dressed man announces. I wonder why he's smiling.

On the way to bed, I step into the rooms of my three sleeping daughters. At the bedside of each I pause and ponder the plight of their future. "What in the world awaits you?" I whisper as I brush back hair and straighten blankets.

Their greatest concerns today are math tests, presents, and birthday parties. Would that their world would always be so innocent. It won't. Forests shadow every trail, and cliffs edge every turn. Every life has its share of fear. My children are no exception.

Nor are yours. And as appealing as a desert island or a monastery might be, seclusion is simply not the answer for facing a scary tomorrow.

Then what is? Does someone have a hand on the throttle of this train, or has the engineer bailed out just as we come in sight of dead-man's curve?

I may have found part of the answer in, of all places, the first chapter of the New Testament. I've often thought it strange that Matthew would begin his book with a genealogy. Certainly not good journalism. A list of who-sired-whom wouldn't get past most editors.

But then again, Matthew wasn't a journalist, and the Holy Spirit wasn't trying to get our attention. He was making a point. God had promised he would give a Messiah through the bloodline of Abraham (Gen. 12:3), and he did.

"Having doubts about the future?" Matthew asks. "Just take a look at the past." And with that he opens the cedar chest of Jesus' lineage and begins pulling out the dirty laundry.

Believe me, you and I would have kept some of these stories in the closet. Jesus' lineage is anything but a roll call at the Institute for Halos and Harps. Reads more like the Sunday morning occupancy at the county jail.

It begins with Abraham, the father of the nation, who more than once lied like Pinocchio just to save his neck (Gen. 20).

Abraham's grandson Jacob was slicker than a Las Vegas card shark. He cheated his brother, lied to his father, got swindled, and then swindled his uncle (Gen. 27, 29).

Jacob's son Judah was so blinded by testosterone that he engaged the services of a streetwalker, not knowing she was his daughter-inlaw! When he learned her identity, he threatened to have her burned to death for solicitation (Gen. 38).

Special mention is made of Solomon's mother, Bathsheba (who bathed in questionable places), and Solomon's father, David, who watched the bath of Bathsheba (2 Sam. 1 i:2-3).

Rahab was a harlot (Josh. 2: 1). Ruth was a foreigner (Ruth 1:4).

Manasseh made the list, even though he forced his children to walk through fire (2 Kings 2 1:6) . His son Amon is on the list, even though he rejected God (2 Kings 21:22).

Seems that almost half the kings were crooks, half were embezzlers, and all but a handful worshiped an idol or two for good measure.

And so reads the list of Jesus' not-so-great grandparents. Seems like the only common bond between this lot was a promise. A promise from heaven that God would use them to send his son.

Why did God use these people? Didn't have to. Could have just laid the Savior on a doorstep. Would have been simpler that way. And why does God tell us their stories? Why does God give us an entire testament of blunders and stumbles of his people?

Simple. He knew what you and I watched on the news last night. He knew you would fret. He knew I would worry. And he wants us to know that when the world goes wild, he stays calm.

Want proof? Read the last name on the list. In spite of all the crooked halos and tasteless gambols of his people, the last name on the list is the first one promised Jesus.

"Joseph was the husband of Mary, and Mary was the mother of Jesus. Jesus is called the Christ" (Mt. 1:16).

Period. No more names are listed. No more are needed. As if God is announcing to a doubting world, "See, I did it. Just like I said I would. The plan succeeded."

The famine couldn't starve it.

Four hundred years of Egyptian slavery couldn't oppress it.

Wilderness wanderings couldn't lose it.

Babylonian captivity couldn't stop it.

Clay-footed pilgrims couldn't spoil it.

The promise of the Messiah threads its way through forty-two generations of rough-cut stones, forming a necklace fit for the King who came. Just as promised.

And the promise remains.

Those people who keep their faith until the end will be saved (Mt. 24:13), Joseph's child assures.

The engineer has not abandoned the train. Nuclear war is no threat to God. Yo-yo economies don't intimidate the heavens. Immoral leaders have never derailed the plan.

God keeps his promise.

See for yourself. In the manger. He's there.

See for yourself. In the tomb. He's gone.[1]

BETWEEN YOU AND GOD

What is your greatest concern for the future?

_____

_____

_____

What would you like to say to the Lord?

_____

_____

_____

_____

_____

_____

---

[1] *When God Whispers Your Name,* pp. 129-133.

SEEING WHAT EYES CAN'T

EPHESIANS 1:19-20
I pray that you will begin to understand how incredibly great his power is to help those who believe him. It is that same mighty power that raised Christ from the dead and seated him in the place of honor at God's right hand in heaven.

I stand six steps from the bed's edge. My arms extended. Hands open. On the bed, Sara–all four years of her—crouches, poised like a playful kitten. She's going to jump. But she's not ready. I'm too close.

"Back more, Daddy," she stands and dares.

I dramatically comply, confessing admiration for her courage. After two giant steps I stop. "More?" I ask.

"Yes!" Sara squeals, hopping on the bed.

With each step she laughs and claps and motions for more. When I'm on the other side of the canyon, when I'm beyond the reach of mortal man, when I am but a tiny figure on the horizon, she stops me. "There, stop there."

"Are you sure?"

"I'm sure," she shouts. I extend my arms. Once again she crouches, then springs. Superman without a cape. Skydiver without a chute. Only her heart flies higher than her body. In that airborne instant her only hope is her father. If he proves weak, she'll fall. If he proves cruel, she'll crash. If he proves forgetful, she'll tumble to the hard floor.

But such fear she does not know, for her father she does. She trusts him. Four years under the same roof have convinced her he is reliable. He is not superhuman, but he is strong. He is not holy, but he is good. He's not brilliant, but he doesn't have to be to remember to catch his child when she jumps.

And so she flies.

And so she soars.

And so he catches her and the two rejoice at the wedding of her trust and his faithfulness.

I stand a few feet from another bed. This time no one laughs. The room is solemn. A machine pumps air into a tired body. A monitor metronomes the beats of a weary heart. The woman on the bed is no child. She was, once. Decades back. She was. But not now.

Like Sara, she must trust. Only days out of the operating room, she's just been told she'll have to return. Her frail hand squeezes mine. Her eyes mist with fear. Unlike Sara, she sees no father. But the Father sees her. Trust him, I say to us both. Trust the voice that whispers your name. Trust the hands to catch.

I sit across the table from a good man. Good and afraid. His fear is honest. Stocks are down. Inflation is up. He has payroll to meet and bills to pay. He hasn't squandered or gambled or played. He has worked hard and prayed often, but now he's afraid. Beneath the flannel suit lies a timid heart.

He stirs his coffee and stares at me with the eyes of Wile E. Coyote when he realizes he's run beyond the edge of a cliff. He's about to fall and fall fast. He's Peter on the water, seeing the storm and not the face. He's Peter in the waves, hearing the wind and not the voice.

Trust, I urge. But the word thuds. He's unaccustomed to such strangeness. He's a man of reason. Even when the kite flies beyond the clouds he still holds the string. But now the string has slipped. And the sky is silent.

I stand a few feet from a mirror and see the face of a man who failed his Maker. Again. I promised I wouldn't, but I did. I was quiet when I should have been bold. I took a seat when I should have taken a stand.

If this were the first time, it would be different. But it isn't. How many times can one fall and expect to be caught?

Trust. Why is it easy to tell others and so hard to remind one's self? Can God deal with death? I told the woman so. Can God deal with debt? I ventured as much with the man. Can God hear yet one more confession from these lips?

The face in the mirror asks.

I sit a few feet from a man on death row. Jewish by birth. Tentmaker by trade. Apostle by calling. His days are marked. I'm curious about what bolsters this man as he nears his execution. So I ask some questions.

Do you have family, Paul? *I have none.*

What about your health? *My body is beaten and tired.*

What do you own? *I have my parchments.* My *pen. A cloak.*

And your reputation? *Well, it's not much. I'm a heretic to some, a maverick to others.*

Do you have friends? *I do, but even some of them have turned back.*

Any awards? *Not on earth.*

Then what do you have, Paul? No belongings. No family. Criticized by some. Mocked by others. What do you have, Paul? What do you have that matters?

I sit back quietly and watch. Paul rolls his hand into a fist. He looks at it. I look at it. What is he holding? What does he have?

He extends his hand so I can see. As I lean forward, he opens his fingers. I peer at his palm. It's empty.

I have my faith. It's all I have. But it's all I need. I have kept the faith.

Paul leans back against the wall of his cell and smiles. And I lean back against another and stare into the face of a man who has learned that there is more to life than meets the eye.

For that's what faith is. Faith is trusting what the eye can't see.

Eyes see the prowling lion. Faith sees Daniel's angel.

Eyes see giants. Faith sees Canaan.

Your eyes see your grave. Your faith sees a city whose builder and maker is God.

Your eyes look in the mirror and see a sinner, a failure, a promise-breaker. But by faith you look in the mirror and see a robed prodigal bearing the ring of grace on your finger and the kiss of your Father on your face.

But wait a minute, someone asks. How do I know this is true? Nice prose, but give me the facts. How do I know these aren't just fanciful hopes?

Part of the answer can be found in Sara's little leaps of faith. Her older sister, Andrea, was in the room watching, and I asked Sara if she would jump to Andrea. Sara refused. I tried to convince her. She wouldn't budge. "Why not?" I asked.

"I only jump to big arms."

If we think the arms are weak, we won't jump.

For that reason, the Father flexed his muscles. "God's power is very great for those who believe," Paul taught. "That power is the same as the great strength God used to raise Christ from the dead" (Eph. 1:19-20 NCV).

Next time you wonder if God can catch you, read that verse. The very arms that defeated death are the arms awaiting you. Next time you wonder if God can forgive you, read that verse. The very hands that were nailed to the cross are open for you.

And the next time you wonder if you will survive the jump, think of Sara and me. If a flesh-and-bone-headed dad like me can catch his child, don't you think your eternal Father can catch you?[1]

BETWEEN YOU AND GOD

How strong do you believe the Father's arms are? Strong enough for you to make a leap of faith?

_____

_____

What would you like to say to the Lord?

_____

_____

_____

_____

_____

_____

---

[1] *When God Whispers Your Name,* pp. 91-96.

JOSEPH'S PRAYER

MATTHEW 1:24
Joseph . . . did what the angel of the Lord had commanded.

The white space between Bible verses is fertile soil for questions. One can hardly read Scripture without whispering, "I wonder. . . ."

"I wonder if Eve ever ate any more fruit."

"I wonder if Noah slept well during storms."

"Did Moses avoid bushes? Did Jesus tell jokes? Did Peter ever try water-walking again?"

The Bible is a fence full of knotholes through which we can peek but not see the whole picture. It's a scrapbook of snapshots capturing people in encounters with God, but not always recording the result. So we wonder:

When the woman caught in adultery went home, what did she say to her husband?

After the demoniac was delivered, what did he do for a living?

After Jairus's daughter was raised from the dead, did she ever regret it?

And Joseph, especially Joseph. I've got questions for Joseph.

Did you and Jesus arm wrestle? Did he ever let you win?

Did you ever look up from your prayers and see Jesus listening?

What ever happened to the wise men?

What ever happened to you?

We don't know what happened to Joseph. His role in Act I is so crucial that we expect to see him the rest of the drama–but with the exception of a short scene with twelve-year-old Jesus in Jerusalem, he never reappears. The rest of his life is left to speculation, and we are left with our questions.

But of all my questions, my first would be about Bethlehem. I'd like to know about the night in the stable. I can picture Joseph there. Moonlit pastures. Stars twinkle above. Bethlehem sparkles in the distance. There he is, pacing outside the stable. He'd made Mary as comfortable as she could be in a barn and then he stepped out. She'd asked to be alone, and Joseph has never felt more so.

In that eternity between his wife's dismissal and Jesus' arrival, what was he thinking? He walked into the night and looked into the stars. Did he pray? For some reason, I don't see him silent; I see Joseph animated, pacing. Head shaking one minute, fist shaking the next. This isn't what he had in mind. I wonder what he said . . . .

This isn't the way I planned it, God. Not at all. My child being born in a stable? This isn't the way I thought it would be. A cave with sheep and donkeys, hay and straw? My wife giving birth with only the stars to hear her pain?

I imagined family. I imagined grandmothers. I imagined neighbors clustered outside the door and friends standing at my side. I imagined the house erupting with the first cry of the infant. Slaps on the back. Loud laughter. Jubilation.

That's how I thought it would be.

This doesn't seem right. What kind of husband am I? I provide no midwife to aid my wife. No bed to rest her back. Her pillow is a blanket from my donkey. My house for her is a shed of hay and straw. The smell is bad, the animals are loud. Why, I even smell like a shepherd myself. Did I miss something? Did I, God?

When you sent the angel and spoke of the son being born–this isn't what I pictured. I envisioned Jerusalem, the temple, the priests, and the people gathered to watch. A pageant perhaps. A parade. A banquet at least. I mean, this is the Messiah!

Out here, what do I have? A weary mule, a stack of fire-wood, and a pot of warm water. This is not the way I wanted it to be! This is not the way I wanted my son.

Oh my, I did it again didn't I, Father? I don't mean to do that; it's just that I forget. He's not my son . . . he's yours. The child is yours. The plan is yours. The idea is yours. And forgive me for asking but . . . is this how God enters the world? The coming of the angel, I've accepted. The questions people asked about the pregnancy, I can tolerate. The trip to Bethlehem, fine. But why a birth in a stable, God?

Any minute now Mary will give birth. Not to a child, but to the Messiah. Not to an infant, but to God. That's what the angel said. That's what Mary believes. And, God, my God, that's what I want to believe. But surely you can understand; it's not easy. It seems so . . . so . . . so . . . bizarre.

I'm unaccustomed to such strangeness, God. I'm a carpenter. I make things fit. I square off the edges. I follow the plumb line. I measure twice before I cut once. Surprises are not the friend of a builder. I like to know the plan.

I like to see the plan before I begin.

But this time I'm not the builder, am I? This time I'm a tool. A hammer in your grip. A nail between your fingers. A chisel in your hands. This project is yours, not mine.

I guess it's foolish of me to question you. Forgive my struggling. Trust doesn't come easy to me, God. But you never said it would be easy, did you?

One final thing, Father. The angel you sent? Any chance you could send another? If not an angel, maybe a person? I don't know anyone around here and some company would be nice. Maybe the innkeeper or a traveler? Even a shepherd would do.

I wonder. Did Joseph ever pray such a prayer? Perhaps he did. Perhaps he didn't.

But you probably have. You've stood where Joseph stood. Caught between what God says and what makes sense. You've done what he told you to do only to wonder if it was him speaking in the first place. You've stared into a sky blackened with doubt.

You've asked if you're still on the right road. You've asked if you were supposed to turn left when you turned right. Things haven't turned out like you thought they would.

Each of us knows what it's like to search the night for light. Not outside a stable, but perhaps outside an emergency room. On the gravel of a roadside. On the manicured grass of a cemetery. We've asked our questions. We questioned God's plan. And we've wondered why God does what he does.

If you are asking what Joseph asked, let me urge you to do what Joseph did. Obey. That's what he did. He obeyed. He obeyed when the angel called. He obeyed when Mary explained. He obeyed when God sent.

He was obedient to God. He was obedient when the sky was bright. He was obedient when the sky was dark.

What about you? Just like Joseph, you can't see the whole picture. Just like Joseph your task is to see that Jesus is brought into your part of your world. And just like Joseph you have a choice: to obey or disobey. Because Joseph obeyed, God used him to change the world.

Can he do the same with you?[1]

BETWEEN YOU AND GOD

Why was important for Joseph to obey even when he did not understand?

_____

_____

What would you like to say to the Lord?

_____

_____

_____

_____

_____

_____

_____

---

[1] *He Still Moves Stones*, pp. 165-170.

GOD UNDER PRESSURE

HEBREWS 4:15
For we have no superhuman High Priest to whom our weaknesses are unintelligible–he himself has shared fully in all our experience of temptation, except that he never sinned. (J. B. Phillips translation)

The writer of Hebrews is adamant almost to the point of redundancy. It's as if he anticipates our objections. It's as if he knows that we will say to God what my friend's son said to him: "God, it's easy for you up there. You don't know how hard it is from down here." So he boldly proclaims Jesus' ability to understand. Look at the wording again.

He himself. Not an angel. Not an ambassador. Not an emissary, but Jesus himself.

Shared fully. Not partially. Not nearly. Not to a large degree. Entirely! Jesus shared fully.

In all our experience. Every hurt. Each ache. All the stresses and all the strains. No exceptions. No substitutes. Why? So he could sympathize with our weaknesses.

A politician dons a hardhat and enters the factory like he is one of the employees. A social worker goes to the inner city and spends the night on the streets with the homeless. A general walks into the mess hall and sits down with the soldiers like he is one of the enlisted men.

All three want to communicate the same message: "I identify with you. I can understand. I can relate." There is one problem, though. The factory employees know that the politician's hardhat will come off when the television crew is gone. The derelicts know that the social worker will be in a warm bed tomorrow night. And the soldiers are well aware that for every meal the general eats in the mess hall, he'll eat dozens in the officers' quarters.

Try as they might, these well-meaning professionals don't really understand. Their participation is partial. Jesus' participation, however, was complete. The writer of Hebrews states with double clarity that Jesus "shared fully in *all* our experience" (emphasis mine).

A bookstore owner in the Northwest once told me about an angry lady who stomped into his store carrying my book, *God Came Near.* She slammed the book on the counter, said a few less-than-kind things about the book, and then screamed loudly enough for everyone on the block to hear, "My God didn't have pimples!"

I know the paragraph that put the spark in her tinderbox. It reads like this:

> Jesus may have had pimples. He may have been tone-deaf. Perhaps a girl down the street had a crush on him
> or vice-versa. It could be that his knees were bony. One thing's for sure: He was, while completely divine,
> completely human."

I can understand why the woman became upset. I can relate to her discomfort. We quickly fix a crack in the stained glass. We rub away any smudges on the altar. There is something *safe* about a God who never had callouses. There is something *awesome* about a God who never felt pain. There is something *majestic* about a God who never scraped his elbow.

But there is also something *cold* about a God who cannot relate to what you and I feel.

If I had a moment with that lady, I would ask her, "Jesus may not have had pimples, but don't you hope that he could have?"

Every page of the Gospels hammers home this crucial principle: God knows how you feel. From the funeral to the factory to the frustration of a demanding schedule. Jesus understands. When you tell God that you've reached your limit, he knows what you mean. When you shake your head at impossible deadlines, he shakes his, too. When your plans are interrupted by people who have other plans, he nods in empathy. He has been there. He knows how you feel."

Let me take you to another day, in a place closer to home. February 15, 1921. New York City. The operating room of the Kane Summit Hospital. A doctor is performing an appendectomy.

In many ways the events leading to the surgery are uneventful. The patient has complained of severe abdominal pain. The diagnosis is clear: an inflamed appendix. Dr. Evan O'Neill Kane is performing the surgery. In his distinguished thirty-seven-year medical career, he has performed nearly four thousand appendectomies, so this surgery will be uneventful in all ways except two.

The first novelty of this operation? The use of local anesthesia in major surgery. Dr. Kane is a crusader against the hazards of general anesthesia. He contends that a local application is far safer. Many of his colleagues agree with him in principle, but in order for them to agree in practice, they will have to see the theory applied.

Dr. Kane searches for a volunteer, a patient who is willing to undergo surgery while under local anesthesia. A volunteer is not easily found. Many are squeamish at the thought of being awake during their own surgery. Others are fearful that the anesthesia might wear off too soon.

Eventually, however, Dr. Kane finds a candidate. The patient is prepped and wheeled into the operating room. A local anesthetic is applied. As he has done thousands of times, Dr. Kane dissects the superficial tissues and locates the appendix. He skillfully excises it and concludes the surgery. During the procedure, the patient complains of only minor discomfort.

The volunteer is taken into post-op, then placed in a hospital ward. He recovers quickly and is dismissed two days later.

Dr. Kane had proven his theory. Thanks to the willingness of a brave volunteer, Kane demonstrated that local anesthesia was a viable, and even preferable, alternative.

But I said there were two facts that made the surgery unique. I've told you the first: the use of local anesthesia. The second is the patient. The courageous candidate for surgery by Dr. Kane was Dr. Kane.

To prove his point, Dr. Kane operated on himself!

A wise move. The doctor became a patient in order to convince the patients to trust the doctor.

I've shared this story with several health professionals. They each gave me the same response: furrowed brow, suspicious grin, and the dubious words, "That's hard to believe."

Perhaps it is. But the story of the doctor who became his own patient is mild compared to the story of the God who became human. But Jesus did. So that you and I would believe that the Healer knows our hurts, he voluntarily became one of us. He placed himself in our position. He suffered our pains and felt our fears.

Rejection? He felt it. Temptation? He knew it. Loneliness? He experienced it. Death? He tasted it. And stress? He could write a best-selling book about it.

Why did he do it? One reason. So that when you hurt, you will go to him–your Father and your Physician–and let him heal.[1]

BETWEEN YOU AND GOD

What are the issues and hurts that you "hide" from the Lord and your brothers in Christ? Why?

_____

_____

_____

What would you like to say to the Lord?

_____

_____

_____

_____

_____

_____

_____

_____

_____

---

[1] *In the Eye of the Storm,* pp. 33-37.

Notes – Week Two

FACE TO FACE
An Encounter with Christ

An Inside Job
Renew Your Mind

AN INSIDE JOB

PSALM 51:10
Create in me a new heart, O God, and renew a steadfast spirit within me.

Spray paint won't fix rust.

A Band-Aid won't remove a tumor.

Wax on the hood won't cure the cough of a motor.

If the problem is inside, you have to go inside.

I learned that this morning. I rolled out of bed early . . . real early. So early that Denalyn tried to convince me not to go to the office. "It's the middle of the night," she mumbled. "What if a burglar tries to break in?"

But I'd been on vacation for a couple of weeks, and I was rested. My energy level was as high as the stack of things to do on my desk, so I drove to the church.

I must confess that the empty streets did look a bit scary. And there was that attempted break-in at the office a few weeks back. So I decided to be careful. I entered the office complex, disarmed the alarm, and then re-armed it so it would sound if anyone tried to enter.

Brilliant, I thought.

I had been at my desk for only a few seconds when the sirens screamed. Somebody is trying to get in! I raced down the hall, turned off the alarm, ran back to my office, and dialed 911. After I hung up, it occurred to me that the thieves could get in before the police arrived. I dashed back down the hall and re-armed the system.

"They won't get me," I mumbled defiantly as I punched in the code.

As I turned to go back to the office, the sirens blared again. I disarmed the alarm and reset it. I could just picture those frustrated burglars racing back into the shadows every time they set off the alarm.

I walked to a window to look for the police. When I did, the alarm sounded a third time. *Hope the police get here soon,* I thought as I again disarmed and reset the alarm.

I was walking back to my office when—that's right—the alarm sounded again. I disarmed it and paused. *Wait a minute; this alarm system must be fouled up.*

I went back to my office to call the alarm company. *Just my luck,* I thought as I dialed. *Of all the nights for the system to malfunction.*

"Our alarm system keeps going off," I told the fellow who answered. "We've either got some determined thieves or a malfunction."

Miffed, I drummed my fingers on my desk as he called up our account.

"There could be one other option," he volunteered.

"What else?"

"Did you know that your building is equipped with a motion detector?"

Oh boy.

About that time I saw the lights from the police car. I walked outside. "Uh, I think the problem is on the inside, not the outside," I told them.

They were nice enough not to ask for details, and I was embarrassed enough not to volunteer any. But I did learn a lesson: You can't fix an inside problem by going outside.

I spent an hour hiding from thieves who weren't there, faulting a system that hadn't failed, and calling for help I didn't need. I thought the problem was out there. All along it was in here.

Am I the only one to ever do that? Am I the only one to blame an inside problem on an outside source?

Alarms sound in your world as well. Maybe not with bells and horns, but with problems and pain. Their purpose is to signal impending danger. A fit of anger is a red flare. Uncontrolled debt is a flashing light. A guilty conscience is a warning sign indicating trouble within. Icy relationships are posted notices announcing anything from neglect to abuse.

You have alarms in your life. When they go off, how do you respond? Be honest, now. Hasn't there been a time or two when you went outside for a solution when you should have gone inward?

Ever blamed your plight on Washington? Inculpated your family for your failure? Called God to account for your problems? Faulted the church for your frail faith?

Reminds me of the golfer about to hit his first shot on the first hole. He swung and missed the ball. Swung again and whiffed again. Tried a third time and still hit nothing but air. In frustration he looked at his buddies and judged, "Man, this is a tough course."

Now, he may have been right. The course may have been tough. But that wasn't the problem. You may be right, as well. Your circumstances may be challenging, but blaming them is not the solution. Nor is neglecting them. Heaven knows you don't silence life's alarms by pretending they aren't screaming. But heaven also knows it's wise to look in the mirror before you peek out the window.

Real change is an inside job. You might alter things a day or two with money and systems, but the heart of the matter is and always will be the matter of the heart.

Allow me to get specific. Our problem is sin. Not finances. Not budgets. Not overcrowded prisons or drug dealers. Our problem is sin. We are in rebellion against our Creator. We are separated from our Father. We are cut off from the source of life. A new president or policy won't fix that. It can only be solved by God.

That's why the Bible uses drastic terms like conversion, repentance, and lost and found. Society may renovate, but only God re-creates.

Here is a practical exercise to put this truth into practice. The next time alarms go off in your world, ask yourself three questions.

1. ***Is there any unconfessed sin in my life?*** (See Ps. 51.)
   Confession is telling God you did the thing he saw you do. He doesn't need to hear it as much as you need to say it. Whether it's too small to be mentioned or too big to be forgiven isn't yours to decide. Your task is to be honest.

2. ***Are there any unresolved conflicts in my world?*** (See Mt. 5:23-24.)
   For example, if you are worshiping and remember that your mom is hacked-off at you for forgetting her birthday, then get off the pew and find a phone. Maybe she'll forgive you; maybe she won't. But at least you can return to your pew with a clean conscience.

3. ***Are there any unsurrendered worries in my heart?*** (See 1 Pet. 5:7.)
   The German word for *worry* means "to strangle." The Greek word means "to divide the mind." Both are accurate. Worry is a noose on the neck and a distraction of the mind, neither of which is befitting for joy.

Alarms serve a purpose. They signal a problem. Sometimes the problem is out there. More often it's in here. So before you peek outside, take a good look inside.[1]

BETWEEN YOU AND GOD

Is there any unconfessed sin in your life? Are there any unresolved conflicts in your world? Are there any unsurrendered worries in your heart?

_____

_____

_____

What would you like to say to the Lord?

_____

_____

_____

_____

_____

_____

_____

_____

---

[1] *When God Whispers Your Name,* pp. 123-128.

THE CHOICE

GALATIANS 5:22-23
But the fruit of the Spirit is love, joy, peace, patience, kindness, goodness, faithfulness, gentleness and self-control. Against such things there is no law.

It's quiet. It's early. My coffee is hot. The sky is still black. The world is still asleep. The day is coming.

In a few moments the day will arrive. It will roar down the track with the rising of the sun. The stillness of the dawn will be exchanged for the noise of the day. The calm of solitude will be replaced by the pounding pace of the human race. The refuge of the early morning will be invaded by decisions to be made and deadlines to be met.

For the next twelve hours I will be exposed to the day's demands. It is now that I must make a choice. Because of Calvary, I'm free to choose. And so I choose.

I choose love . . . .

No occasion justifies hatred; no injustice warrants bitterness. I choose love. Today I will love God and what God loves.

I choose joy . . . .

I will invite my God to be the God of circumstance. I will refuse the temptation to be cynical . . . the tool of the lazy thinker. I will refuse to see people as anything less than human beings, created by God. I will refuse to see any problem as anything less than an opportunity to see God.

I choose peace . . . .

I will live forgiven. I will forgive so that I may live.

I choose patience . . . .

I will overlook the inconveniences of the world. Instead of cursing the one who takes my place, I'll invite him to do so. Rather than complain that the wait is too long, I will thank God for a moment to pray. Instead of clinching my fist at new assignments, I will face them with joy and courage.

I choose kindness . . . .

I will be kind to the poor, for they are alone. Kind to the rich, for they are afraid. And kind to the unkind, for such is how God has treated me.

I choose goodness . . . .

I will go without a dollar before I take a dishonest one. I will be overlooked before I will boast. I will confess before I will accuse. I choose goodness.

I choose faithfulness . . . .

Today I will keep my promises. My debtors will not regret their trust. My associates will not question my word. My wife will not question my love. And my children will never fear that their father will not come home.

I choose gentleness . . . .

Nothing is won by force. I choose to be gentle. If I raise my voice may it be only in praise. If I clench my fist, may it be only in prayer. If I make a demand, may it be only of myself.

I choose self-control . . . .

I am a spiritual being. After this body is dead, my spirit will soar. I refuse to let what will rot, rule the eternal. I choose self-control. I will be drunk only by joy. I will be impassioned only by my faith. I will be influenced only by God. I will be taught only by Christ. I choose self-control.

Love, joy, peace, patience, kindness, goodness, faithfulness, gentleness, and self-control. To these I commit my day. If I succeed, I will give thanks. If I fail, I will seek his grace. And then, when this day is done, I will place my head on my pillow and rest.[1]

---

[1] *When God Whispers Your Name*, pp. 71-73.

BETWEEN YOU AND GOD

Have you made time each morning to choose how you want to live that day? Why or why not?

_____

_____

_____

What would you like to say to the Lord?

_____

_____

_____

_____

_____

_____

_____

_____

_____

_____

_____

_____

_____

_____

_____

_____

_____

_____

TURNING YOURSELF IN

1 JOHN 1:9
If we confess our sins, he will forgive our sins, because we can trust God to do what is right. He will cleanse us from all the wrongs we have done.
JAMES 5:16
Confess your sins to each other and pray for each other so that God can heal you.

Charles Robertson should have turned himself in. Not that he would've been acquitted; he robbed a bank. But at least he wouldn't have been the laughingstock of Virginia Beach.

Cash-strapped Robertson, nineteen, went to Jefferson State Bank on a Wednesday afternoon, filled out a loan application, and left. Apparently he changed his mind about the loan and opted for a quicker plan. He returned within a couple of hours with a pistol, a bag, and a note demanding money. The teller complied, and all of a sudden Robertson was holding a sack of loot.

Figuring the police were fast on their way, he dashed out the front door. He was halfway to the car when he realized he'd left the note. Fearing it could be used as evidence against him, he ran back into the bank and snatched it from the teller. Now holding the note and the money, he ran a block to his parked car. That's when he realized he'd left his keys on the counter when he'd returned for the note.

"At this point," one detective chuckled, "total panic set in."

Robertson ducked into the restroom of a fast-food restaurant. He dislodged a ceiling tile and hid the money and the .25 caliber handgun. Scampering through alleys and creeping behind cars, he finally reached his apartment where his roommate, who knew nothing of the robbery, greeted him with the words, "I need my car."

You see, Robertson's getaway vehicle was a loaner. Rather than confess to the crime and admit the bungle, Robertson shoveled yet another spade of dirt deeper into the hole. "Uh, uh, your car was stolen," he lied.

While Robertson watched in panic, the roommate called the police to inform them of the stolen vehicle. About twenty minutes later an officer spotted the "stolen" car a block from the recently robbed bank. Word was already on the police radio that the robber had forgotten his keys. The officer put two and two together and tried the keys on the car. They worked.

Detectives went to the address of the person who'd reported the missing car. There they found Robertson. He confessed, was charged with robbery, and put in jail. No bail. No loan. No kidding.

Some days it's hard to do anything right. It's even harder to do anything wrong right. Robertson's not alone. We've done the same. Perhaps we didn't take money but we've taken advantage or taken control or taken leave of our senses and then, like the thief, we've taken off. Dashing down alleys of deceit. Hiding behind buildings of work to be done or deadlines to be met. Though we try to act normal, anyone who looks closely at us can see we are on the lam:

Eyes darting and hands fidgeting, we chatter nervously. Committed to the cover-up, we scheme and squirm, changing the topic and changing direction. We don't want anyone to know the truth, especially God.

But from the beginning God has called for honesty. He's never demanded perfection, but he has expected truthfulness.

Confession does for the soul what preparing the land does for the field. Before the farmer sows the seed he works the acreage, removing the rocks and pulling the stumps. He knows that seed grows better if the land is prepared. Confession is the act of inviting God to walk the acreage of our hearts. "There is a rock of greed over here Father, I can't budge it. And that tree of guilt near the fence? Its roots are long and deep. And may I show you some dry soil, too crusty for seed?" God's seed grows better if the soil of the heart is cleared.

Confession admits wrong and seeks forgiveness; amnesty denies wrong and claims innocence.

Many mouth a prayer for forgiveness while in reality claiming amnesty. Consequently our worship is cold (why thank God for a grace we don't need?) and our faith is weak (I'll handle my mistakes myself, thank you). We are better at keeping God out than we are at inviting God in. Am I missing the mark when I say that many of us attend church on the run? Am I out of line when I say many of us *spend life on the run?*

Am I overstating the case when I announce, "Grace means you don't have to run anymore!"? It's the truth. Grace means it's finally safe to turn ourselves in.

Peter did. Remember Peter? "Flash the sword and deny the Lord" Peter? The apostle who boasted one minute and bolted the next? He snoozed when he should have prayed. He denied when he should have defended. He cursed when he should have comforted. He ran when he should have stayed. We remember Peter as the one who turned and fled, but do we remember Peter as the one who returned and confessed? We should.

I've got a question for you.

How did the New Testament writers know of his sin? Who told them of his betrayal? And, more importantly, how did they know the details? Who told them of the girl at the gate and the soldiers starting the fire? How did Matthew know it was Peter's accent that made him a suspect? How did Luke learn of the stare of Jesus? Who told all four of the crowing rooster and flowing tears?

The Holy Spirit? I suppose. Could be that each writer learned of the moment by divine inspiration. Or, more likely, each learned of the betrayal by an honest confession. Peter turned himself in. Like the bank robber, he bungled it and ran. Unlike the robber, Peter stopped and thought. Somewhere in the Jerusalem shadows he quit running, fell to his knees, buried his face in his hands, and gave up.

But not only did he give up, he opened up. He went back to the room where Jesus had broken the bread and shared the wine. (It says a lot about the disciples that they let Peter back in the door.)

How can I be so sure? Two reasons.

I.) *He couldn't stay away*. Here is a good rule of thumb: Those who keep secrets from God keep their distance from God. Those who are honest with God draw near to God. Confessed sin becomes the bridge over which we can walk back into the presence of God.

2.) *He couldn't stay silent*. Only fifty days after denying Christ, Peter is preaching Christ. This is not the action of a fugitive. What took him from traitor to orator? He let God deal with the secrets of his life. "Confess your sins to each other and pray for each other so that God can heal you" (James 5:16). The fugitive lives in fear, but the penitent lives in peace.

May I ask a frank question? Are you keeping any secrets from God? Any parts of your life off limits? Any cellars boarded up or attics locked? Any part of your past or present that you hope you and God never discuss?

Learn a lesson from the robber: The longer you run, the worse it gets. Learn a lesson from Peter: The sooner you speak to Jesus, the more you'll speak for Jesus. Once you're in the grip of grace, you're free to be honest. Turn yourself in before things get worse. You'll be glad you did.

Honest to God, you will.[1]

BETWEEN YOU AND GOD

Are you keeping any secrets from God? Any parts of your life off limits?

_____

_____

_____

What would you like to say to the Lord?

_____

_____

_____

_____

_____

_____

---

[1] Adapted from *In the Grip of Grace,* pp. 119-127.

LOOK BEFORE YOU LABEL

MATTHEW 7:1-2
Don't judge other people, or you will be judged. You will be judged in the same way you judge others, and the amount you give to others will be given to you (NCV).

Recently we took our kids on a vacation to a historical city. While going on a tour through an old house, we followed a family from New York City. They didn't tell me they were from New York. They didn't have to. I could tell. They wore New York City clothes. Their teenager had one half of his head shaved and on the other half of his head, his hair hung past his shoulders. The daughter wore layered clothes and long beads. The mother looked like she'd raided her daughter's closet, and the dad's hair was down the back of his neck.

I had them all figured out. The kid was probably on drugs. The parents were going through a midlife crisis. They were rich and miserable and in need of counseling. Good thing I was nearby in case they wanted spiritual counsel.

After a few moments they introduced themselves. I was right; they were from New York City. But that is all I got right. When I told them my name, they were flabbergasted. "We can't believe it!" they said. "We've read your books. We use them in our Sunday school class in church. I tried to get over to hear you when you spoke in our area, but that was our family night and . . . ."

Sunday school? Church? Family night? Oh, boy. I'd made a mistake. A big mistake. I'd applied the label before examining the contents.

We've all used labels. We stick them on jars and manila folders so we'll know what's inside. We also stick them on people for the same reason.

John tells of a time the disciples applied a label. Jesus and his followers came upon a man who had been blind from birth. Here is the question the disciples asked Jesus: "Teacher, whose sin caused this man to be born blind–his own sin or his parents' sin?" (Jn. 9:2).

Never mind that the man is a beggar in need of help. Never mind that the man has spent his life in a dark cave. Never mind that the man seated in front of them is in earshot of their voices. Let's talk about his sin.

How could they be so harsh? So insensitive? So . . . blind.

The answer? (You may not like it.) It's easier to talk about a person than to help a person. It's easier to debate homosexuality than to be a friend to a gay person. It's easier to discuss divorce than to help the divorced. It's easier to argue abortion than to support an orphanage. It's easier to complain about the welfare system than to help the poor.

It's easier to label than to love.

It's especially easy to talk theology. Such discussions make us feel righteous. Self-righteous.

Is that to say religious discussion is wrong? Of course not. Is that to say we should be unconcerned for doctrine or lax in a desire for holiness? Absolutely not. That is to say there is something wrong with applying the label before examining the contents. Do you like it when people label you before they know you?

"So, you're unemployed?" (Translation: *Must be a bum.*)

"Hmm, you're an accountant?" (Translation: *Must be dull.*)

"She's an Episcopalian." (Translation: *Must be liberal.*)

"She's an Episcopalian who voted for the democrats." (Translation: *Must be liberal beyond help.*)

"Oh, I'm sorry; I didn't know you were a divorcee." (Translation: *Must be immoral.*)

"He's a fundamentalist." (Translation: *Narrow-minded half-wit.*)

Labels. A fellow gave me one the other day. We got into a lively discussion about some ethical issues. Somewhere in our conversation he asked me what kind of work I was in. I told him I was minister, and he said, "Oh, I see," and grew silent.

I wanted to say, "No, you don't. Don't you put me in that box. I'm not a minister. I am Max-who-ministers. Don't you put me in that box with all those hucksters and hypocrites you may know. That's not fair."

Labels. So convenient. Stick them on a person, and you know what pantry to use.

What if God did that with us? What if God judged us by our outward appearance? What if he judged us based on where we grew up? Or what we do for a living? Or the mistakes we made when we were young? He wouldn't do that, would he?

"Don't judge other people, or you will be judged. You will be judged in the same way you judge others, and the amount you give to others will be given to you" (Matt. 7:1-2). Be careful when you judge. That doesn't mean we shouldn't discern. That does mean we shouldn't pass the verdict. The amount of grace you give is the amount you get.

Jesus had another view of the man born blind. Rather than see him as an opportunity for discussion, he saw him as an opportunity for God. Why was he blind? "So God's power could be shown in him" (John 9:3).

What a perspective! The man wasn't a victim of fate; he was a miracle waiting to happen. Jesus didn't label him. He helped him. Jesus was more concerned about the future than the past.

Who do you best relate to in this story? Some of you relate to the man born blind. You have been the topic of conversation. You have been left on the outside looking in. You've been labeled.

If so, learn what this man learned: When everyone else rejects you, Christ accepts you. When everyone else leaves you, Christ finds you. When no one else wants you, Christ claims you. When no one else will give you the time of day, Jesus will give you the words of eternity.

Others of you will relate to the observers. You've judged. You've labeled. You've slammed the gavel and proclaimed the guilt before knowing the facts. If that is you, go back to John 9:4 and understand what the work of God is: "While it is daytime we must continue doing the work of the One who sent me."

What is the work of God? Accepting people. Loving before judging. Caring before condemning.

Look before you label.[1]

BETWEEN YOU AND GOD

How would those closest to you describe you—judging or caring?

_____

_____

_____

What would you like to say to the Lord?

_____

_____

_____

_____

_____

_____

_____

_____

_____

_____

_____

_____

_____

_____

_____

_____

[1] Adapted from *A Gentle Thunder*, pp. 157-160.

THE CIVIL WAR OF THE SOUL

ROMANS 7:9-10
Once I was alive apart from law; but when the commandment came, sin sprang to life and I died. I found that the very commandment that was intended to bring life actually brought death.

ROMANS 7:21-24
So I find this law at work: When I want to do good, evil is right there with me. For in my inner being I delight in God's law; but I see another law at work in the members of my body, waging war against the law of my mind and making me a prisoner of the law of sin at work within my members. What a wretched man I am! Who will rescue me from this body of death?

My felonious actions began innocently. My route to the office takes me south to an intersection where I and every other person in Texas turn east. Each morning I wait long minutes in a long line at a long light, always mumbling, "There must be a better way." A few days back I found it. While still a half-mile from the light, I spotted a shortcut, an alley behind a shopping center. It was worth a try. I turned on my blinker, made a quick left, bid farewell to the crawling commuters, and took my chances. I weaved in between the dumpsters and over the speed bumps and voila. It worked! The alley led me to my eastbound avenue several minutes faster than the rest of society.

Lewis and Clark would have been proud. I certainly was. From then on, I was ahead of the pack. Every morning while the rest of the cars waited in line, I veered onto my private autobahn and smugly applauded myself for seeing what others missed. I was surprised that no one had discovered it earlier, but then again, few have my innate navigational skills.

One morning Denalyn was with me in the car. "I'm about to remind you why you married me," I told her as we drew near to the intersection. "See that long line of cars? Hear that dirge from the suburbs? See that humdrum of humanity? It's not for me. Hang on!"

Like a hunter on a safari, I swerved from the six-lane onto the one-lane and shared with my sweetheart my secret expressway to freedom. "What do you think?" I asked her, awaiting her worship.

"I think you broke the law."

"What?"

"You just went the wrong way on a one-way street."

"I did not."

"Go back and see for yourself."

I did. She was right. Somehow I'd missed the sign. My road-less-taken was a route-not-permitted. Next to the big orange dumpster was a "Do Not Enter" sign. No wonder people gave me those looks when I turned into the alley. I thought they were envious; they thought I was deviant.

But my problem is not what I did before I knew the law. My problem is what I want to do now, after I know the law. You'd think that I would have no desire to use the alley, but I do! Part of me still wants the shortcut. Part of me wants to break the law. (Forgive me all you patrolmen who are reading this.) Each morning the voices within me have this argument:

My "ought to" says, "It's Illegal."

My "want to" answers, "But I've never been caught."

My "ought to" reminds, "The law is the law."

My "want to" counters, "But the law isn't for careful drivers like me. Besides, the five minutes I save I'll dedicate to prayer."

My "ought to" doesn't buy it. "Pray in the car."

Before I knew the law, I was at peace. Now that I know the law, an insurrection has occurred. I'm a torn man. On one hand I know what to do, but I don't want to do it. My eyes read the sign "Do Not Enter," but my body doesn't want to obey. What I should do and end up doing are two different matters. I was better off not knowing the law.

Sound familiar? It could. For many it is the itinerary of the soul. Before coming to Christ we all had our share of shortcuts. Immorality was a shortcut to pleasure. Cheating was a shortcut to success. Boasting was a shortcut to popularity. Lying was a shortcut to power.

Then we found Christ, we found grace, and we saw the signs. Hasn't it happened to you? You've got a hot temper and then read, "If you are angry with a brother or sister, you will be judged" (Mt. 5:22 NCV). WOW, I *never knew that.*

You've got wandering eyes and then read, "If anyone looks at a woman and wants to sin sexually with her, in his mind he has already done that sin with the woman" (Mt. 5:28 NCV). *Oh my, now what do I do?*

You enjoy letting people see your generosity and then read, "So when you give to the poor, don't let anyone know what you are doing" (Mt. 6:3 NCV). *Oh boy, I didn't know that was wrong.*

All these years you've been taking shortcuts, never seeing the "Do Not Enter" sign. But now you see it. Now you know it. So what do you do?

These are the questions of Romans 7. And these are the questions of many Christians. Maybe you've hit your head against the wall. Are there weaknesses within you that stun you? Your words? Your thoughts? Your temper? Your greed? Your grudge? Your gossip? Things were better before you knew the law existed. But now you know. And now you have a war to wage. And I have two truths about grace for you to take into battle.

1. He still claims you.

Remember your position–you are a child of God. Some interpret the presence of the battle as the abandonment of God. That's Satan sowing those seeds of shame. "God's tired of your struggles," he whispers. "Your father is weary of your petitions for forgiveness," he lies. And many believe him, spending years convinced that they are disqualified from the kingdom and do not deserve to ask for forgiveness again.

Forgive my abrupt response, but who told you that you deserved forgiveness the first time? When you came to Christ did he know every sin you'd committed up until that point? Yes. Did Christ know every sin you would commit in the future? Yes, he knew that too. So Jesus saved you, knowing all the sins you would ever commit until the end of your life? Yes. You mean he is willing to call you his child even though he knows each and every mistake of your past and future? Yes.

2. He still guides you

When under attack, our tendency is to question the validity of God's commands; we rationalize like I do with the one-way street. *The law is for others, not for me. I'm a good driver.* By questioning the validity of the law, I decrease in my mind the authority of the law.

Our city lawmakers' thoughts are not like my thoughts. They are concerned for the public good. I am concerned with personal convenience. They want what is best for the city. I want what is best for me. They know what is safe. I know what is quick. But they don't create laws for my pleasure; they make laws for my safety.

The same is true with God. What we consider shortcuts God sees as disasters. He doesn't give laws for our pleasure. He gives them for our protection. In seasons of struggle we must trust his wisdom, not ours. He designed the system; he knows what we need.

Why are we so quick to revert back to our old ways? Simply stated: We are helpless to battle sin alone. Aren't we glad Paul answered his own question? "I thank God for saving me through Jesus Christ our Lord!" (v. 25).

The same One who saved us first is there to save us still.

There is never a point at which you are any less saved than you were the first moment he saved you. When you lost your temper yesterday, you didn't lose your salvation. Your name doesn't disappear and reappear in the book of life according to your moods and actions. Such is the message of grace.

You are saved, not because of what you do, but because of what Christ did. And you are special, not because of what you do, but because of whose you are. And you are his.

And because we are his, let's forget the shortcuts and stay on the main road. He knows the way. He drew the map.[1]

BETWEEN YOU AND GOD

How does it help you to know that every Christian fights in internal battle with sin?

_____

_____

_____

---

[1] Adapted from *In the Grip of Grace*, pp. 139-148.

What would you like to say to the Lord?

_____
_____
_____
_____
_____
_____
_____
_____
_____
_____
_____
_____

Notes – Week Three

_____
_____
_____
_____
_____
_____
_____
_____
_____
_____
_____
_____
_____
_____
_____
_____
_____

FACE TO FACE

An Encounter with Christ

POST-RETREAT DEVOTIONAL
WEEK FOUR

Extending Your Arms

Love One Another

THE CAVE PEOPLE

JOHN 8:12
When Jesus spoke again to the people, he said, "I am the light of the world. Whoever follows me will never walk in darkness, but will have the light of life.

Long ago, or maybe not so long ago, there was a tribe in a dark, cold cavern. The cave dwellers would huddle together and cry against the chill. Loud and long they wailed. It was all they did. It was all they knew to do. The sounds in the cave were mournful, but the people didn't know it, for they had never known joy. The spirit in the cave was death, but the people didn't know it, for they had never known life.

But then, one day, they heard a different voice. "I have heard your cries," it announced. "I have felt your chill and seen your darkness. I have come to help."

The cave people grew quiet. They had never heard this voice. Hope sounded strange to their ears. "How can we know you have come to help?"

"Trust me," he answered. "I have what you need."

The cave people peered through the darkness at the figure of the stranger. He was stacking something, then stooping and stacking more.

"What are you doing?" one cried, nervous.

The stranger didn't answer.

"What are you making?" one shouted even louder.

Still no response.

"Tell us!" demanded a third.

The visitor stood and spoke in the direction of the voices. "I have what you need." With that he turned to the pile at his feet and lit it. Wood ignited, flames erupted, and light filled the cavern.

The cave people turned away in fear. "Put it out!" they cried. "It hurts to see it."

"Light always hurts before it helps," he answered. "Step closer. The pain will soon pass."

"Not I," declared a voice.

"Nor I," agreed a second.

"Only a fool would risk exposing his eyes to such light."

The stranger stood next to the fire. "Would you prefer the darkness? Would you prefer the cold? Don't consult your fears. Take a step of faith."

For a long time no one spoke. The people hovered in groups covering their eyes. The fire builder stood next to the fire. "It's warm here," he invited.

"He's right," one from behind him announced. "It's warmer." The stranger turned and saw a figure slowly stepping toward the fire. "I can open my eyes now," he proclaimed. "I can see."

"Come closer," invited the fire builder.

He did. He stepped into the ring of light. "It's so warm!" He extended his hands and sighed as his chill began to pass.

"Come, everyone! Feel the warmth," he invited.

"Silence, man!" cried one of the cave dwellers. "Dare you lead us into your folly? Leave us. Leave us and take your light with you."

He turned to the stranger. "Why won't they come?"

"They choose the chill, for though it's cold, it's what they know. They'd rather be cold than change."

"And live in the dark?"

"And live in the dark."

The now-warm man stood silent. Looking first at the dark, then at the visitor.

"Will you leave the fire?" the stranger asked.

The man paused, then answered, "I cannot. I cannot bear the cold." Then he spoke again. "But nor can I bear the thought of my people in darkness."

"You don't have to," the fire builder responded, reaching into the fire and removing a stick. "Carry this to your people. Tell them the light is here, and the light is warm. Tell them the light is for all who desire it."

And so the man took the small flame and stepped into the shadows.[1]

---

[1] Adapted from *A Gentle Thunder,* pp. 181-183.

BETWEEN YOU AND GOD

Who are the "cave people" in your life? Are you willing to share the light of life with them?

_____

_____

_____

What would you like to say to the Lord?

_____

_____

_____

_____

_____

_____

_____

_____

_____

_____

_____

_____

_____

_____

_____

_____

SEEDS OF PEACE

JAMES 3:18
Those who are peacemakers will plant seeds of peace and reap a harvest of goodness. (TLB)

Want to see a miracle? Try this.

Take a seed the size of a freckle. Put it under several inches of dirt. Give it enough water, light, and fertilizer. And get ready. A mountain will be moved. It doesn't matter that the ground is a zillion times the weight of the seed. The seed will push it back.

Every spring, dreamers around the world plant tiny hopes in overturned soil. And every spring, their hopes press against impossible odds and blossom.

Never underestimate the power of a seed.

As far as I know, James, the epistle writer, wasn't a farmer. But he knew the power of a seed sown in fertile soil. The principle for peace is the same as the principle for crops: Never underestimate the power of a seed.

How good are you at sowing seeds of peace?

You may not be called on to ward off international conflict, but you will have opportunities to do something more vital: to bring *inner* peace to troubled hearts.

Jesus modeled this. We don't see him settling many disputes or negotiating conflicts. But we do see him cultivating inward harmony through acts of love:

washing the *feet of* men he knew would betray him,

having lunch with a corrupt tax official,

honoring the sinful woman whom society had scorned.

He built bridges by healing hurts. He prevented conflict by touching the interior. He cultivated harmony by sowing seeds of peace in fertile hearts.

Do me a favor. Pause for a moment and think about the people who make up your world. Take a stroll through the gallery of faces that are significant to you. Mentally flip through the scrapbook of snapshots featuring those you deal with often.

Can you see their faces? Your spouse. Your best friend. Your golf buddies. Your friends at PTA. Your kids. Your aunt across the country. Your neighbor across the street. The receptionist at work. The new secretary in the next office.

Freeze-frame those mental images for a moment while I tell you how some of them are feeling.

I went to our family doctor not long ago. I went for my first check-up since the one required for high school football seventeen years ago.

Since I was way overdue, I ordered the works. One nurse put me on a table and stuck little cold suction cups to my chest. Another nurse wrapped a heavy band around my arm and squeezed a black bulb until my arm tingled. Then they pricked my finger (which always hurts) and told me to fill up a cup (which is always awkward). Then, with all the preliminaries done, they put me in a room and told me to take off my shirt and wait on the doctor.

There is something about being poked, pushed, measured, and drained that makes you feel like a head of lettuce in the produce department. I sat on a tiny stool and stared at the wall.

May I tell you something you know, but may have forgotten? Somebody in your world feels like I felt in that office. The daily push and shove of the world has a way of leaving us worked over and worn out. Someone in your gallery of people is sitting on a cold aluminum stool of insecurity, clutching the backside of a hospital gown for fear of exposing what little pride he or she has left. And that person desperately needs a word of peace.

Someone needs you to do for them what Dr. Jim did for me.

Jim is a small-town doctor in a big city. He still remembers names and keeps pictures of babies he delivered on his office bulletin board. And though you know he's busy, he makes you feel you are his only patient.

After a bit of small talk and a few questions about my medical history, he put down my file and said, "Let me take off my doctor hat for a minute and talk to you as a friend."

The chat lasted maybe five minutes. He asked me about my family. He asked me about my work load. He asked me about my stress. He told me he thought I was doing a good job at the church and that he loved to read my books.

Nothing profound, nothing probing. He went no deeper than I allowed. But I had the feeling he would have gone to the bottom of the pit with me had I needed him to.

After those few minutes, Dr. Jim went about his task of tapping my knee with his rubber hammer, staring down my throat, looking in my ear, and listening to my chest. When he was all done, as I was buttoning up my shirt, he took his doctor hat off again and reminded me not to carry the world on my shoulders. "And be sure to love your wife and hug those kids, because when it all boils down to it, you're not much without them."

"Thanks, Jim," I said.

And he walked out as quickly as he'd come in–a seed sower in a physician's smock.

Want to see a miracle? Plant a word of love heartdeep in a person's life. Nurture it with a smile and a prayer, and watch what happens.

An employee gets a compliment. A wife receives a bouquet of flowers. A cake is baked and carried next door. A widow is hugged. A gas-station attendant is honored. A preacher is praised.

Sowing seeds of peace is like sowing beans. You don't know why it works; you just know it does. Seeds are planted, and topsoils of hurt are shoved away.[1]

BETWEEN YOU AND GOD

Have you sown any seeds of peace lately? Name one or two people you know who needs one.

_____

_____

_____

What would you like to say to the Lord?

_____

_____

_____

_____

_____

_____

_____

_____

_____

_____

_____

_____

_____

_____

---

[1] *The Applause of Heaven*, pp. 141-146.

THE PHOTO AND THE FILE

MATTHEW 5:9
Blessed are the peacemakers, for they will be called sons of God.

This morning I began the process of decision. I opened the "Decision File" and began reading the speaking invitations. A church planter in Wyoming wonders if I could spend time with his church. A church camp in Washington invites me to speak to its campers. A missionary in India has read my books and asks, "If I can come up with the money, can you spend a week with us?"

Something happens as a person fields the invitations of others. He or she begins to feel important.

As I looked at the letters, it dawned on me how vital I was to the progress of humanity.

I wondered how the earth stayed on its axis before I was born. I nodded my head in understanding at the letter that read, "You are the one for this meeting." I put my hand under my shirt and rubbed the S on the red jersey–"Super Max."

I was feeling puffy and proud when I read the last letter. But as I put down the file, I noticed another request. One that didn't make it into the folder. One that was lying on my desk.

It had no date, no signature, no deadline. It wasn't a letter or a phone message. It was a photograph–a photograph so recent that it had no frame. It was a portrait of a mom and a dad encircled by three little girls. Our family portrait.

The positioning of the photo and the file struck me. There was something symbolic about the way I'd unintentionally placed the letters next to the family picture. The singular photo lying in the shadow of the stack of requests seemed to whisper a question that only I could answer:

"Max, who will win?"

There is only so much sand in the hourglass. Who gets it?

You know what I'm talking about, don't you? Since you don't stockpile your requests, your situation may not be as graphic as mine. But it's every bit as real.

"There's going to be some shuffling in the ranks. With the retirement of the branch manager, *somebody will* move up. The company is looking for a bright, young salesman—someone like you—who is willing to demonstrate his dedication to the organization by taking on some extra projects . . . and working some late hours."

"Would I be willing to serve as chapter president? Well, to be honest, I was going to sit out this term because our youngest goes to college next fall. Yes, I realize this is a critical year for the organization . . . . Oh, no, I wouldn't want the club to falter . . . . Yes, we have made great progress over the last few months. It's just that . . ."

It's tug-of-war, and you are the rope.

On one side are the requests for your time and energy. They call. They compliment. They are valid and good. Great opportunities to do good things. If they were evil, it'd be easy to say no. But they aren't, so it's easy to rationalize.

On the other side are the loved ones in your world. They don't write you letters. They don't ask you to consult your calendar. They don't offer to pay your expenses. They don't use terms like "appointment," "engagement," or "do lunch." They don't want you for what you can do for them; they want you for who you are.

Clovis Chappell, a minister from a century back, used to tell the story of two paddleboats. They left Memphis about the same time, traveling down the Mississippi River to New Orleans. As they traveled side by side, sailors from one vessel made a few remarks about the snail's pace of the other.

Words were exchanged. Challenges were made. And the race began. Competition became vicious as the two boats roared through the Deep South.

One boat began falling behind. Not enough fuel. There had been plenty of coal for the trip, but not enough for a race. As the boat dropped back, an enterprising young sailor took some of the ship's cargo and tossed it into the ovens. When the sailors saw that the supplies burned as well as the coal, they fueled their boat with the material they had been assigned to transport. They ended up winning the race, but burned their cargo.

God has entrusted cargo to us, too: children, spouses, friends. Our job is to do our part in seeing that this cargo reaches its destination. Yet when the program takes priority over people, people often suffer.

How much cargo do we sacrifice in order to achieve the number one slot? How many people never reach the destination because of the aggressiveness of a competitive captain?

As I looked at the photo and the file, I decided to try something. I decided to make a list of what I would lose by saying no to my family one night. It wasn't hard to do; I just made a list of what I would have missed by not being home with my family last night.

I could have been out of town this week. I had an invitation to be in the Midwest at a church. I turned it down. What if I hadn't? If I had gone, I would have had the attention of a thousand people for an hour. I would have had the opportunity to speak about Jesus to some people who don't know him. Is a Tuesday evening at home with three children and a spouse more important than preaching to an audience?

Read my list of what I would have missed. Then you decide.

I would have missed a trip to the swimming pool in which I saw Jenna climb onto her inner tube for the first time.

I would have missed fifteen minutes of bouncing up and down in the shallow end of the pool, with Andrea clinging to my neck singing the theme from "Sleeping Beauty."

I would have missed seeing Denalyn get sentimental as she unpacked a box of baby clothes.

I wouldn't have gone on a walk with the girls during which Jenna found ten "special" rocks.

I wouldn't have been there to hold Andrea when her finger got slammed in the door.

I wouldn't have been there to answer Jenna's question: "Daddy, what is a handicapped person?"

I would have missed seeing Andrea giggle as she took Jenna's straw when Jenna's back was turned.

I wouldn't have heard Jenna tell the story of Jesus on the cross during our family devotional (when she assured us, "But he didn't stay dead!").

I wouldn't have seen Andrea make a muscle with her arm and sing, "Our God is so BIIIIIIG!"

What do you think? I know my vote. There are a hundred speakers who could have addressed that crowd, but my girls just have one daddy.

After I made my list, just for the fun of it I picked up the phone and called the church that had asked me to come and speak this week. The minister wasn't in, but his secretary was. "Isn't this the week of your seminar?" I asked.

"Oh, yes! It has been a wonderful success!"

They didn't even miss me.

Now I've got a better idea what to do with my stack of requests.[1]

BETWEEN YOU AND GOD

Do you have a hard time saying no to demands on your time? What could you do to increase the time you spend on your highest priorities?

_____

_____

What would you like to say to the Lord?

_____

_____

_____

_____

_____

_____

[1] *In the Eye of the Storm,* pp. 95-100.

WHEN FISHERMEN DON'T FISH

MARK 1:17
"Come, follow me," Jesus said, "and I will make you fishers of men."

When I was in high school, our family used to fish every year during spring break. One year my brother and my mom couldn't go, so my dad let me invite a friend. I asked Mark. He was a good pal and a great sport. He got permission from his parents, and we began planning our trip.

Days before leaving, we could already anticipate the vacation. We could feel the sun warming our bodies as we floated in the boat. We could feel the yank of the rod and hear the spin of the reel as we wrestled the white bass into the boat. And we could smell the fish frying in an open skillet over an open fire.

We could hardly wait. Days passed like cold molasses. Finally spring break arrived. We loaded our camper and set out for the lake.

We arrived late at night, unfolded the camper, and went to bed—dreaming of tomorrow's day in the sun. But during the night, an unseasonably strong norther blew in. It got cold fast! The wind was so strong that we could barely open the camper door the next morning. The sky was gray. The lake was a mountain range of white-topped waves. There was no way we could fish in that weather.

"No problem," we said. "We'll spend the day in the camper. After all, we have Monopoly. We have *Reader's Digest.* We all know a few jokes. It's not what we came to do, but we'll make the best of it and fish tomorrow."

So, huddled in the camper with a Coleman stove and a Monopoly board, we three fishermen passed the day—indoors. The hours passed slowly, but they did pass. Night finally came, and we crawled into the sleeping bags dreaming of angling.

Were we in for a surprise. The next morning it wasn't the wind that made the door hard to open, it was the ice!

We tried to be cheerful. "No problem," we mumbled. "We can play Monopoly . . . again. We can reread the stories in *Reader's Digest.* And surely we know another joke or two." But as courageous as we tried to be, it was obvious that some of the gray had left the sky and entered our camper.

I began to notice a few things I hadn't seen before. I noticed that Mark had a few personality flaws. He was a bit too cocky about his opinions. He was easily irritated and constantly edgy. He couldn't take any constructive criticism. Even though his socks did stink, he didn't think it was my business to tell him.

"Just looking out for the best interest of my dad's camper," I defended, expecting Dad to come to my aid.

But Dad just sat over in the corner, reading. *Humph,* I thought, *where is he when I need him?* And then, I began to see Dad in a different light. When I mentioned to him that the eggs were soggy and the toast was burnt, he invited me to try my hand at the portable stove. *Touchy, touchy, I* said to myself. *Nothing like being cooped up an a camper with someone to help you see his real nature.*

It was a long day. It was a long, cold night.

When we awoke the next morning to the sound of sleet slapping the canvas, we didn't even pretend to be cheerful. We were flat-out grumpy. Mark became more of a jerk with each passing moment; I wondered what spell of ignorance I must have been in when I invited him. Dad couldn't do anything right; I wondered how someone so irritable could have such an even-tempered son. We sat in misery the whole day, our fishing equipment still unpacked.

The next day was even colder. "We're going home" were my father's first words. No one objected.

I learned a hard lesson that week. Not about fishing, but about people.

When those who are called to fish don't fish, they fight.

When energy intended to be used outside is used inside, the result is explosive. Instead of casting nets, we cast stones. Instead of extending helping hands, we point accusing fingers. Instead of being fishers of the lost, we become critics of the saved. Rather than helping the hurting, we hurt the helpers.

The result? Church Scrooges. "Bah humbug" spirituality. Beady eyes searching for warts on others while ignoring the warts on the nose below. Crooked fingers that bypass strengths and point out weaknesses.

Split churches. Poor testimonies. Broken hearts. Legalistic wars.

And, sadly, poor go unfed, confused go uncounseled, and lost go unreached.

When those who are called to fish don't fish, they fight.

But note the other side of this fish tale: When those who are called to fish, fish—they flourish!

Nothing handles a case of the gripes like an afternoon service project. Nothing restores perspective better than a visit to a hospital ward. Nothing unites soldiers better than a common task.

Leave soldiers inside the barracks with no time on the front line and see what happens to their attitude. The soldiers will invent things to complain about. Bunks will be too hard. Food will be too cold. Leadership will be too tough. The company will be too stale. Yet place those same soldiers in the trench and let them duck a few bullets, and what was a boring barracks will seem like a haven. The beds will feel great. The food will be almost ideal. The leadership will be courageous. The company will be exciting.

When those who are called to fish, fish–they flourish!

Make a note of that. The next time the challenges "outside" tempt you to shut the door and stay inside, stay long enough to get warm. Then get out. When those who are called to fish don't fish, they fight.[1]

BETWEEN YOU AND GOD

What is your very best "fish" story? How long has it been since you last caught one?

_____

_____

_____

What would you like to say to the Lord?

_____

_____

_____

_____

_____

_____

_____

_____

_____

_____

_____

_____

_____

_____

---

[1] *In the Eye of the Storm*, pp. 55-58.

FOREVER YOUNG

LUKE 17:33
Whoever tries to keep his life safe will lose it, and the man who is prepared to lose his life will preserve it (Phillips).

Don't you hate it when someone else reminds you? The barber: "Getting a little thin on top here, Joe."
The invitation: "You are invited to your thirtieth high school reunion.
Your kids: "Tell me again, who were the Rolling Stones?"
Your doctor: "Nothing to worry about, Bill. Your condition is common for folks in their mid-age."
The dawning of old age. The first pages of the final chapters. A golden speck appears on the green leaves of your life, and you are brought face to wrinkled face with the fact that you are getting older.
And though we joke ("Old age is when you sink your teeth into a steak . . . and they stay there"), not everyone laughs. Especially one who has been taught to treasure youth.
And weren't we all?
For decades you worried about everything except getting old. Out of all the things you couldn't count on, there was one thing you could, and that was your youth. You could eat like a horse and not look like one. All the schoolteachers were older than you. Professional athletes were about the same age as your older brother. Life was an open highway, and death was a millennium away.
But then they came, the subtle messages of mortality:
You buy your first life insurance policy and it includes burial and funeral expenses. Your carpool friends ask you why you squint when you read road signs.
At first it's just raindrop reminders splashing on your watercolor convictions of perpetual youth. With time, however, the raindrops become steady and stronger.
Everything hurts when you wake up. What doesn't hurt, doesn't work. Your parents begin acting like your children. The smile lines don't go away when you stop smiling.
And then–boom! The rain becomes a torrent. The gentle taps become thunder. Cardiac arrest. Empty nest. Forty candles. Bifocals. Boom. Boom! BOOM!
Now there is no denial. Ponce de Leon didn't find the fountain of youth, and neither will you. Oh, but how we try. Barbells get pumped. Black hair gone gray goes black again, or better yet, blond. The van is traded in on a truck, a four-wheel-drive monster that will tackle the treacherous ravines of the interstate. The face gets stretched. The chin gets tucked.
But try as we might, the calendar pages still turn. The clocks still tick. And the body still grows older. And with every new pill we take we are reminded that growing old is a pill that has to be swallowed.
But why does the pill go down so slowly? Why is it so hard to accept? Certainly part of the problem is the mirror (or at least the reflection in it). Time, as they say, is a great healer, but it's a lousy beautician.
Or, for others, there is failure. What you set out to do, you didn't. You set out to avoid the trap of suburbia; now you're making mortgage payments. You determined to leave a legacy, but all you've left so far is a trail of diapers and check stubs.
But the real pain is deeper. For some it is the hollowness of success. Life at the top of the ladder can be lonely. Mahogany desks grow cold. Sales awards tarnish. Diplomas fade. Sometimes a dream-come-true world has come true and it's less than you'd hoped.
Regret becomes a major pastime. The plumber wishes he'd gone to medical school and the doctor wishes he were a plumber. It can get even worse. Regret can lead to rebellion. Rebellion against the demands. Rebellion against the mundane. Rebellion against the ho-hum. Rebellion against whatever ties you down: your job, your government, your station wagon, or worse still . . . your family.
Those who rebel–those who choose to roam the back alleys of escape–are prime candidates to stumble into one of Satan's oldest pits . . . adultery.
A pretty, young secretary from down the hall brings some papers as well as some sympathy into your office . . .
The David in us calls for Bathsheba. Potiphar's wife looks at Joseph. A romp is taken in the greener grass and the hurt begins.
Let me be very clear with my point: Growing old can be dangerous. The trail is treacherous and the pitfalls are many. One is wise to be prepared. You know it's coming. It's not like God kept the process a secret. It's not like you are blazing a trail as you grow older. It's not as if no one has ever done it before. Look around you. You have ample

opportunity to prepare and ample case studies to consider. If growing old catches you by surprise, don't blame God. He gave you plenty of warning. He also gave you plenty of advice.

Want some examples? Glad you asked. How about Luke 17:33? "Whoever tries to keep his life safe will lose it, and the man who is prepared to lose his life will preserve it" (Phillips).

"There are two ways to view life," Jesus is saying, "those who protect it or those who pursue it. The wisest are not the ones with the most years in their lives, but the most life in their years."

There is a rawness and a wonder to life. Pursue it. Hunt for it. Sell out to get it. Don't listen to the whines of those who have settled for a second-rate life and want you to do the same so they won't feel guilty. Your goal is not to live long; it's to live.

Jesus says the options are clear. On one side there is the voice of safety. You can build a fire in the hearth, stay inside, and stay warm and dry and safe. You can't be criticized for what you don't try, right? You can't fall if you don't take a stand, right? You can't lose your balance if you never climb, right? So, don't try it. Take the safe route.

Or you can hear the voice of adventure–God's adventure. Instead of building a fire in your hearth, build a fire in your heart. Follow God's impulses. Adopt the child. Move overseas. Teach the class. Change careers. Run for office. Make a difference. Sure it isn't safe, but what is?

Reclaim the curiosity of your childhood. Just because you're near the top of the hill doesn't mean you've passed your peak. Your last chapters can be your best. Your final song can be your greatest. It could be that all of your life has prepared you for a grand exit. God's oldest have always been among his choicest.

It was his octogenarian activities that got Moses into your Bible. Old and mellow Abraham was much wiser than young and brash Abram. Caleb still claimed his mountain when he was eighty-five. And look at John, the aged apostle John. The dear friend of Jesus. Surely his final years will be quiet and restful. Surely John has done what he came to do.

Nope. Don't tell that to John. And don't tell that to God. For neither of them was finished. John had one more chapter to write. What was intended to be an island of isolation became a place of inspiration, and in his final years John wrote the final book of the Bible. Could it be that all of John's life had led to this moment?

The final years can be your best. As we get older, our vision should improve. Not our vision of earth but our vision of heaven. Time slips. Days pass. Years fade. And life ends. And what we came to do must be done while there is time.

We would think it bizarre for a traveler not to be prepared for the end of the journey. We would pity the poor passenger who never read his itinerary. We'd be bewildered by someone who thought the purpose of the trip was the trip.

Others, however, are anticipating the destination. I hope you are. And I hope you'll be ready when you get home. For you, age is no enemy. Age is a mile–marker-a gentle reminder that home has never been so near.

Tell that to your barber.[1]

BETWEEN YOU AND GOD

Name some current reminders of your mortality.

_____

_____

_____

---

[1] Adapted from *He Still Moves Stones,* pp. 63-69.

What would you like to say to the Lord?

_____

_____

_____

_____

_____

_____

_____

_____

_____

_____

_____

Notes – Week Four

_____

_____

_____

_____

_____

_____

_____

_____

_____

_____

_____

_____

_____

_____

FACE TO FACE

MEN'S SMALL-GROUP BIBLE STUDIES

As iron sharpens iron,
so one man sharpens another.
PROVERBS 27:17

INTRODUCTION
Men's Small-Group Bible Studies

A sign of growth in the world of nature is change—change in the dimensions of a tree, fruit appearing on the vine, and flowers blooming in the garden. In a similar way, change for us means new levels of maturity, of understanding, and in the way we relate to our family and friends—truly being a Promise Keeper.

But what does it take for change to occur? In one word, time. Not just the ticking of the clock, but time that is given purposefully in this next year to study God's Word with brothers in Christ and become accountable to each other. Your life will be re-engineered week by week in the hour you invest in the group. The goal is not to make you a Bible scholar, but to help you learn to live with Jesus Christ as the center of your life, one day at a time. Each weekly session is designed to take **one hour**.

> ➢ Open with fellowship around coffee and friendship (**about 10 minutes**).
> ➢ Then allow **40 minutes** to interact with the biblical material. The questions for each session are answered interactively in the group.
> ➢ Use the final **10 minutes** for application and prayer.

This may be your first time to participate in a weekly small group that meets for fellowship, Bible study, and prayer. Some men are hesitant to get involved simply because they're not sure where the group is going. In this case, we're seeking to take the next step from the retreat to the small group. When men gather in the name of Jesus Christ, Almighty God is pleased. And when they gather weekly to fellowship, pray, and apply God's Word, measurable change takes place. So pick a place to meet, and go for it!

LEADER'S GUIDELINES

Leaders of small-group Bible studies have traditionally been people of superior biblical knowledge and (hopefully) great spiritual maturity. But in Promise Builders small groups, we're changing some of the rules. Our leaders are meant to be facilitators, not biblical experts. The purpose of the Promise Builder group leader is to encourage discussion and interaction. Thus, he is more a coach than a commentator. In other words, the group is meant to be leader-light. There are, however, a few responsibilities for the leader:

> ➢ Start and end each session on time. This shows respect for the men and their duties.
> ➢ Pray for group members by name before each meeting.
> ➢ Value each man's comments and insights.

The meeting can take place most anywhere, but we suggest a room like the back of a restaurant, a cafeteria, a conference room, a community center, or someone's office. Work closely with the men who are facilitating the group in other ways, such as the timekeepers, the prayer leader, and the calendar coordinator. These simple guidelines, plus the carrier-group mindset described below, will help you and the other men in your group begin to see life-changing results as you go through the studies in this book.

THE BEST APPROACH FOR YOUR GROUP
Several Patterns of Men's Small-Group Bible Studies

Men who gather in a small group to fellowship, study the Bible, and pray together predictably follow one of several patterns. Often they aren't even aware of the dynamic of their group, since they're accustomed to it. Of course, the leader of the group has tremendous influence in this area. The best dynamic for these particular Bible studies may require some changes in the way you do things (if yours is an established group). But hopefully, you'll see the benefits of becoming a group that majors on interactive discussion and application of the timeless insights of God's Word.

"Adrift"–The Life Raft Group. This small group is made up of survivors–men who have survived a major battle in their lives. It may have been a recent battle or one from years ago. But the wounds and scars are reminders of what each has suffered. What began as an emergency situation has turned into a weekly meeting. So each man is just happy to be among his friends. Life raft groups really have no leader–each man has his own story to tell around some biblical idea or paragraph. Of concern to the men is that they're adrift. And though high on encouragement, they're low on long-term biblical resources.

"Feeling Good"–The Yacht Group. If you long to feel good among friends, climb aboard this craft! The skipper will welcome you with a hot cup of coffee or whatever else you'd like. Each man needs a Bible, of course–and the study will begin as soon as they push off. But meanwhile, just enjoy the Lord and each other. For some reason, the seagoing stories of fellow mariners always take more time than the skipper planned for, so time in the Word will resume next week. Your need to move beyond the fellowship–to get into the Word–may we urge you on to see what other boats are in the harbor?

"Battle Weary"–The Destroyer Group. This pattern is named after the naval vessel of the same class. It's a warship, armed and ready for battle against the forces of evil in society and our lives. Disciplined Bible study is the order of the day. Truth from Scripture is fired from the leader like missiles from the deck launchers. Some of the sailors look as if they took direct hits from the Word, but the leader has properly warned them that such are the costs of discipleship. No one questions the reality of spiritual warfare, though the battle-weary men sense the need for some spiritual support from the Lord.

"Deep and Long: Where Are We?"—The Submarine Group. To the captain of the sub, there are just two kinds of boats: subs and targets. Aboard this kind of small group, Bible study gives the experience of going down deep, staying down long, and, after a while, wondering where you really are. A life of disciplined study is essential if you're to last with this group. And you may not be sure the captain likes you, but you know you're investing time in a highly strategic activity, below the surface of life. If it's fellowship balanced with interactive Bible study and prayer you're looking for, however, you'd better not go down the ladder into the sub group.

"Refreshed, Refueled, Refocused"—The Carrier Group. An aircraft carrier is a warship equipped with a large open deck for the taking off and landing of war-planes. As well, it's equipped to carry, service, and arm its planes. A small group Bible study in this pattern is on a mission, underway to be in strategic position for the men on board. Each time the men come in, in the midst of the work week, they know they will be refreshed, refueled, and refocused for life's battles and open seas. They leave ready to fulfill the biblical plan they studied, alert to serve their Captain well. This kind of small group is best for the sessions ahead.

POWER TO CHANGE[1]
Men's Small-Group Bible Study

GETTING BETTER AT ANY SPORT USUALLY REQUIRES MORE TIME THAN WE'RE WILLING TO SPEND. THOSE WHO HAVE ACHIEVED EXCELLENCE IN BASKETBALL, FOOTBALL, SOCCER, BOWLING, RACQUETBALL, OR GOLF HAVE DONE SO AT GREAT PERSONAL SACRIFICE. ANY ATHLETE WHO HAS PLAYED A SPORT VERY LONG HAS PICKED UP UNDESIRABLE HABITS HOWEVER. WHEN HE SEES HIS GAME NEEDING CHANGES HE SEEKS HELPFUL RESOURCES.

WHAT KINDS OF BAD HABITS DO ATHLETES GET INTO?

WHAT RESOURCES WOULD YOU SUGGEST?

BACKGROUND

When it comes to change in our lives, no one can do a more thorough job than God Himself. A case in point is the apostle Peter, one of God's great trophies. The changes in him were measurable and tasting.

CONSIDER THIS

"YOU CHRISTIANS SHOULD DWELL ON ONE THING—JESUS CHRIST CHANGES LIVES.

IN EVERY STUDENT IN MY CLASS WHO HAS BECOME A CHRISTIAN AND WHOM I HAVE OBSERVED, I HAVE SEEN A CHANGED LIFE."

University Philosophy Professor

ACTION POINT

What one thing would I like God to change today?

_____

_____

_____

........READ........

JOHN 13:36-38; 18:15-27

QUESTIONS FOR INTERACTION

1. Why was Peter so confident that he would not deny his Lord? Why did **he** fail so miserably?

2. What kinds of things do so many guys want to change in their lives but without much success?

........READ........

Acts 4:1-14

3. What was different now about Peter?

4. What explains this change?

5. You may know someone whose life has been dramatically changed by the Spirit of God. How have most observers attempted to explain the changes?

WRAP-UP:

EVERY GOLFER'S DREAM IS TO PLAY A ROUND WITH A PRO LIKE JACK NICKLAUS. BETTER YET, WHAT IF "THE GOLDEN BEAR" WERE TO CLIMB INSIDE YOU AND ACTUALLY PLAY HIS GAME THROUGH YOU? EVERY ASPECT OF YOUR GAME WOULD BE POWERFULLY CHANGED! ALTHOUGH THAT'S NOT REALITY IT IS TRUE THAT GODS SPIRIT LIVES IN YOU AND DESIRES TO LIVE THE LIFE OF JESUS THROUGH YOU. EACH MAN ANSWER: IF THE HOLY SPIRIT WERE TO EMPOWER YOUR LIFE, WHAT CHANGES COULD YOU EXPECT FROM HIM?

---

[1] *Applying the Seven Promises,* Promise Keepers, Word Publishing, Nashville, 1996, pp. 28-29.

UNDER THE CIRCUMSTANCES[1]
Men's Small-Group Bible Study

WARM-UP:

"A SHIPLOAD OF VIETNAM-BOUND YOUNG SAILORS DESPERATELY NEEDS A CHAPLAIN. WE ALL WALKED UP THE GANGPLANK TOGETHER, BUT I KNEW THAT I WAS RESPONSIBLE FOR WHAT THESE YOUNG MEN WOULD DO WITH THE FEARS AND WORRIES THAT ONLY WAR CAN BRING. I WAS SOUNDLY AWARE THAT MY OWN EMOTIONS NEEDED PROTECTION AS WELL. WE STUDIED THE SCRIPTURES AND PRAYED TOGETHER ON THAT LONG FLOAT ACROSS THE SEAS, AND WE DISCOVERED AN AMAZING CALM. IN FACT, I DO NOT PERSONALLY REMEMBER A SINGLE NIGHT'S REST IN MY ONE-YEAR ASSIGNMENT WHEN MY SLEEP WAS INTERRUPTED BY FEAR." **U.S. Navy Chaplain**

HOW DO YOU TEND TO RESPOND TO TRYING CIRCUMSTANCES (E.G., WITH YOUR FINANCES, FAMILY, JOB SECURITY, WORK ASSOCIATES)? WHAT HAVE YOU FOUND TO CALM YOUR FEARS?

BACKGROUND

Sensing that there's a design to the order of the Psalms, today's selection moves us from the sweeping view of life and nations we find in Psalms 1 and 2 to an issue of daily reality. How do we handle the fears, foes, and frustrations that come our way as we try to follow the Lord?

David wrestled with this, as we all do. But Psalm 3 is more than a rehearsal of woes. The great king and warrior will model the way we can respond when surrounded by overwhelming circumstances.

CONSIDER THIS

DR. HOWARD HENDRICKS TELLS OF GREETING A BROTHER WITH, "HOW ARE YOU?"
THE MAN RESPONDED, "WELL, UNDER THE CIRCUMSTANCES..."
DR. HENDRICKS WAS QUICK TO ASK, "WHAT ARE YOU DOING UNDER THERE?"

ACTION POINT

In light of this psalm, what are some steps I can take to move out from under my circumstances?

_____

_____

_____

........READ.........

📖   **PSALM 3**

QUESTIONS FOR INTERACTION

1. Why was David under his circumstances in this psalm?

2. What good is a shield when under attack?

3. Why would the king need his head lifted?

4. People in distress often have trouble sleeping. How could David sleep while surrounded by his adversaries?

5. Once the king's personal fears were quieted, what did he need God to do? (v. 7; see also 2 Chron. 21:3 and Prov. 21:31)

6. Why such contrast between verses 1 and 8?

WRAP-UP:

IF SOMEONE UNDER THE CIRCUMSTANCES FEELS HELPLESS, HOPELESS, AND WORTHLESS, HOW WILL THIS PSALM LIFT HIS HEAD? EACH MAN CHOOSE ONE WORD TO DESCRIBE A CIRCUMSTANCE THAT IS PRESENTLY PULLING HIM DOWN.

---

[1] Promise Keepers, *Applying the Seven Promises,* Word Publishing, Nashville, 1996, pp. 44-45.

SWIMSUIT EDITION[1]
Men's Small-Group Bible Study

THE ATLANTA AIRPORT IS A LONG WAY FROM JACK'S HOME OR ANYONE HE KNOWS. *SPORTS ILLUSTRATED'S* NEW SWIMSUIT EDITION HAS JUST HIT THE NEWSSTAND, AND IT CATCHES HIS EYE AS HE WALKS TOWARD GATE 1-13. STANDING IN FRONT OF THE NEWSPAPERS, HIS EYES ARE REALLY ON THE SPECIAL S.I. EDITION. WITHIN MINUTES, JACK IS SITTING IN A VACANT GATE AREA WITH A NEW MAGAZINE AND A FRESH APPRECIATION FOR THE LATEST SWIMSUITS.

HOW COULD JACK HAVE RESISTED THAT TEMPTATION?

BACKGROUND

The universal appeal of the Psalms for their comfort, wisdom, and insight into the ways of the Lord is readily felt in this gateway selection for today's study. The two paths of life—the way of the godly and the way of the sinful—are clearly in view. Likely we think we're on the first pathway. But do we really know what are its regimens and benefits? Likewise, the consequences of the way of the sinful are often under-estimated.

CONSIDER THIS

SALES OF SOFT-PORN MAGA-ZINES GROSSED $1 MILLION A YEAR FOR RICHDALE'S, A CHAIN OF 53 FAMILY CONVENIENCE STORES IN NEW ENGLAND. BUT THE VICE PRESIDENT OF OPERATIONS DIDN'T THINK THE MAGAZINES WERE APPRO-PRIATE— SO HE PULLED THEM.

CITIZEN
NOVEMBER 21, 1994

ACTION POINT

How can I get the Word of God to be more attrac-tive to me than *Sports Illustrated's* swimsuit edition?

_____
_____
_____

........READ.........

PSALM 1

QUESTIONS FOR INTERACTION

1. What is the downward progression of verse 1? How do we see this pattern in today's warm-up?

2. How do we get the desire to "delight in the law of the Lord"?

3. What do you think the psalmist had in mind when he said, "And in His law he meditates day and night"?

4. What are the results when we delight in and meditate on the Word? (v.3)

5. What if we don't?

6. What comfort do you find in verse 6?

DESCRIBE ONE PERSON YOU KNOW WHO HAS TRAVELED THE DOWNWARD PATH AND ANOTHER WHO CHOSE THE UPWARD PATH (NO NAMES, PLEASE). EACH MAN NAME ONE HABIT HE CAN DEVELOP TO PROTECT HIMSELF FROM THE DOWNWARD PATH.

---

[1] *Applying the Seven Promises,* Promise Keepers, Word Publishing, Nashville, 1996, pp. 40-41.

"LIKE A GOOD NEIGHBOR"[1]
Men's Small-Group Bible Study

WARM-UP:

WE LIVE IN COMMUNITIES TODAY WHERE WE HARDLY KNOW OUR NEIGHBORS. OUR WORLD SEEMS IMPERSONAL BECAUSE OF OUR PACE OF LIFE, AND IN A SENSE, WE'RE AFRAID TO GET INVOLVED IN THE LIVES OF PEOPLE.

WHAT QUALITIES DO YOU LOOK FOR IN A GOOD FRIEND OR NEIGHBOR?

BACKGROUND

A neighbor is commonly thought to be the person next door. In the time of the New Testament, however, neigh-bor commonly meant "one living in the same land." Thus, a neighborhood in those days might well have included a number of villages.

CONSIDER THIS

"THE GOOD YOU DO TODAY WILL BE FORGOTTEN TOMOR-ROW. DO GOOD ANYWAY."
Anonymous

ACTION POINT

What seems to keep me from getting involved in the needs of others, especially those of other cultural back-grounds?

_____

_____

_____

_____

I desire to become avail-able to a brother in need this coming week. His name is:

_____

......READ.........

 LUKE 10:25-37

QUESTIONS FOR INTERACTION

1. What give us reason to think this attorney did not love his neighbor? (v.29)

2. Agree/disagree: As long as I don't know who my neighbor is, I have no responsibility to him. Explain your answer:

3. What did the first two men who encountered this man have in common? Why didn't they stop and help?

4. What motivated the Samaritan to stop and help? What builds compassion in a life?

5. If we were traveling the freeway to Jericho, what might keep us from stopping?

6. Under what conditions would you have stopped to help?

7. What does it mean to be a neighbor according to Jesus?

WRAP-UP:

IF SOMEONE UNDER THE CIRCUMSTANCES FEELS HELPLESS, HOPELESS, AND WORTHLESS, HOW WILL THIS PSALM LIFT HIS HEAD? EACH MAN CHOOSE ONE WORD TO DESCRIBE A CIRCUMSTANCE THAT IS PRESENTLY PULLING HIM DOWN.

---

[1] *Applying the Seven Promises*, pp. 26-27.

BIBLIOGRAPHY

Horner, Bob, Ron Ralston, and Dave Sunde. *Promise Builders Study Series*: *Applying the Seven Promises*. Nashville: Word Publishing, 1996.

Lucado, Max. *A Gentle Thunder*. Nashville: Word Publishing, 1995.

Lucado, Max. *The Applause of Heaven*. Nashville: Word Publishing, 1990, 1996, 1999.

Lucado, Max. *He Still Moves Stones*. Nashville: Word Publishing, 1993, 1999.

Lucado, Max. *In the Eye of the Storm*. Nashville: Word Publishing, 1991.

Lucado, Max. *In the Grip of Grace*. Nashville: Word Publishing, 1996.

Lucado, Max. *Just Like Jesus*. Nashville: Word Publishing, 1998.

Lucado, Max. *When Christ Comes*. Nashville: Word Publishing, 1999.

Lucado, Max. *When God Whispers Your Name*. Nashville: Word Publishing, 1994, 1999.

APPLYING THE SEVEN PROMISES
Bob Horner, Ron Ralston, and David Sunde

These application studies encourage men to honor God and integrate his Word into all their relationships by incorporating the power of worship, prayer and mentoring to daily life. A key resource for men's small group study or for personal growth.

THE MAKING OF A GODLY MAN WORKBOOK
John Trent

Designed specifically to help men in their pursuit of a deeper, more abiding faith in God, this in-depth study offers a plan for integrating the seven promises of a Promise Keeper into everyday life. Insightful and practical, *The Making of a Godly Man* is a great tool for men's groups or individual study.

PROMISE KEEPER AT WORK
Bob Homer, Ron Ralston, and David Sunde

In 45 easy-to-use study sessions, *The Promise Keeper at Work* teaches men how to integrate their faith, as well as a higher ethical standard, into the workplace. With biblical guidelines and practical applications, this book is packed full of wisdom and insight that will give work and life new purpose.

SEVEN PROMISES OF A PROMISE KEEPER
Various Authors

This best-selling book has been completely revised and expanded with new author insights and stories on each of the Promise Keeper's seven promises. Men will find practical ways to deepen their Christian walk with encouraging chapters from Bill Bright, James Dobson, Gary Smalley, Luis Palau and many others.

SEVEN PROMISES PRACTICED
Various Authors

Based on the video series of the same title, *Seven Promises Practiced* offers a wealth of knowledge and insights outlining the Promise Keepers' seven promises for Christian men. With teaching from well-known leaders such as Jack Hayford, Gary Smalley, Charles Swindoll and Max Lucado,
(Study Guide also available.)

SEVEN PROMISES PRACTICED
Video Series

This seven-video series shows how to unlock the power and potential of men and how to cultivate life-changing relationships with family and friends.

Speakers include:
Jack Hayford, Howard Hendricks, Crawford Loritts, Gary Smalley, Charles R. Swindoff, Max Lucado, and Isaac Canales.

OTHER EZ LESSON PLANS

The EZ Lesson Plan was designed with the facilitator in mind. This new format gives you the flexibility as a teacher to use the video as the visual and then refer to the facilitator's guide for the questions….and even better, the answers. It is designed for a four-week study, communicated by our top authors and it is totally self contained. **Each EZ Lesson Plan requires the student's guides to be purchased separately as we have maintained a very low purchase price on the video resource.**

Please visit your local Christian bookstore to see the other titles we have available in the EZ Lesson Plan format. We have listed some of the titles and authors for your convenience:

EZ LESSON PLANS NOW AVAILABLE:

The 10 Commandments of Dating   Ben Young and Dr. Samuel Adams
AVAILABLE NOW

Are you tired of pouring time, energy, and money into relationships that start off great and end with heartache? If so, you need *The 10 Commandments of Dating* to give you the hard-hitting, black-and-white, practical guidelines that will address your questions and frustrations about dating. This guide will help you keep your head in the search for the desire of your heart.
EZ Lesson Plan ISBN: 0-7852-9619-0   Student's Guide ISBN: 0-7852-9621-2

Extreme Evil: Kids Killing Kids   Bob Larson
AVAILABLE NOW

Kids are killing kids in public schools! Kids are killing their parents! What is causing all of this evil in our younger generation? Do we need prayer back in the schools…or do we need God to start in the home? Bob Larson gets us to the root of these evils and brings us some of the answers we are looking for in this new video assisted program.
EZ Lesson Plan ISBN: 0-7852-9701-4   Student's Guide ISBN: 0-7852-9702-2

Life Is Tough, but God Is Faithful   Sheila Walsh
AVAILABLE NOW

Sheila takes a look at eight crucial turning points that can help you rediscover God's love and forgiveness. Showing how the choices you make affect your life, she offers insights from the book of Job, from her own life, and from the lives of people whose simple but determined faith helped them become shining lights in a dark world.
EZ Lesson Plan ISBN: 0-7852-9618-2   Student's Guide ISBN: 0-7852-9620-4

Why I Believe

D. James Kennedy

AVAILABLE NOW

In this video, Dr. D. James Kennedy offers intelligent, informed responses to frequently heard objections to the Christian faith. By dealing with topics such as the Bible, Creation, the Resurrection and the return of Christ, *Why I Believe* provides a solid foundation for Christians to clarify their own thinking while becoming more articulate in the defense of their faith.

EZ Lesson Plan ISBN: 0-8499-8770-9   **Student's Guide ISBN: 0-8499-8769-5**

The Lord's Prayer

Jack Hayford

AVAILABLE NOW

Why do we say "Thy Kingdom come?" What does "Hallowed be Thy Name" mean? Do we really practice "Forgive us our debts as we forgive our debtors?" Pastor Jack Hayford walks you through verse by verse and then applies his great scripture insights to our personal lives. This study will put "meaning to the words" you have just been saying for years.

EZ Lesson Plan ISBN: 0-7852-9442-2   **Student's Guide ISBN: 0-7852-9609-3**

How To Pray

Ronnie Floyd

AVAILABLE NOW

Whether you are a rookie in prayer or a seasoned prayer warrior, this video kit will meet you where you are and take you to another level in your prayer life. You may have been raised in a Christian home where prayer was a normal, daily exercise. You may have attended church all of your life, where the prayers of the people and the minister were as common as the hymns that still ring in your ears. Yet such experiences do not guarantee that you know how to pray. With simple, yet profound prose, Dr. Floyd declares, "prayer occurs when you depend on God, prayerlessness occurs when you depend on yourself."

EZ Lesson Plan ISBN: 0-8499-8790-3   **Student's Guide ISBN: 0-8499-8793-8**

Healing Prayer

Reginald Cherry, M.D.

AVAILABLE NOW

"Prayer is the divine key that unlocks God's pathway to healing in both the natural and supernatural realms of life." In Healing Prayer, Dr. Cherry explores the connection between faith and healing, the Bible and medicine. He blends the latest research, true stories, and biblical principles to show that spirit-directed prayers can bring healing for disease.

EZ Lesson Plan ISBN: 0-7852-9666-2   **Student's Guide ISBN: 0-7852-9667-0**

Jesus and The Terminator
Jack Hayford
AVAILABLE NOW

From the **E-Quake** Series comes the EZ Lesson Plan that is the focal point of the Book of Revelation. Pastor Hayford sets the stage for the fight against the Evil One when the end of time comes upon us. There is no greater force than that of Jesus and now viewers will see Him become triumphant again in this battle that is evident.

EZ Lesson Plan ISBN: 0-7852-9601-8   Student's Guide ISBN: 0-7852-9658-1

The Law of Process
John C. Maxwell
AVAILABLE NOW

Leadership develops daily, not in a day. This law, taken from **The Twenty One Irrefutable Laws of Leadership**, is the first of the series to be placed into an individual study. Take each opportunity as it comes along and find the answer in a way only strong leaders would do it….by processing it. John explains how and why "Champions don't become champions in the ring…they are merely recognized there."

EZ Lesson Plan ISBN: 0-7852-9671-9   Student's Guide ISBN: 0-7852-9672-7

Forgiveness
John MacArthur
AVAILABLE NOW

In this three-session EZ Lesson Plan, noted biblical scholar John MacArthur provides an insightful look at forgiveness. MacArthur not only reminds us that we are called to grant forgiveness to those who sin against us, but he also teaches the importance of learning to accept the forgiveness of others.

EZ Lesson Plan ISBN: 0-8499-8808-X   Student's Guide ISBN: 0-8499-8809-8

Andy Griffith Volume 1 Bible Study Series
Systems Media, Inc.
AVAILABLE NOW

For generations, stories have been used to teach universal truths. In keeping with this time-honored tradition, the new three-volume Andy Griffith Bible Study Series has been developed, which uses the classic stories of Mayberry to illustrate biblical truths. In *Honesty*, the first volume of the series, learn from Andy, Opie, and the gang as they struggle with, and learn from, everyday life situations.

EZ Lesson Plan ISBN: 0-8499-8815-2   Student's Guide ISBN: 0-8499-8816-0

Created To Be God's Friend
Henry Blackaby
AVAILABLE NOW

Henry Blackaby being born a man of God, living his life as a man of God, teaches us how all of us are created equal in being God's friend. No Christian need live without a keen sense of purpose, and no believer need give up on finding daily closeness with God.

EZ Lesson Plan ISBN: 0-7852-9718-9   Student's Guide ISBN: 0-7852-6758-1

The Murder of Jesus

John MacArthur

AVAILABLE AUGUST 22, 2000

To many, the story of Christ's crucifixion has become so familiar that it has lost its ability to shock, outrage or stir any great emotion. In *The Murder of Jesus*, John MacArthur presents this pivotal moment in the life of Jesus in a way that forces the viewers to witness this event in all its power. The passion of Christ is examined chronologically through the lens of the New Testament with special attention given to Jesus' words on the cross, the miracles that attended the crucifixion, and the significance of Christ's atoning work.

EZ Lesson Plan ISBN: 0-8499-8796-2   **Student's Guide ISBN: 0-8499-8797-0**

Fresh Brewed Life

Nicole Johnson

AVAILABLE SEPTEMBER 5, 2000

God is calling us to wake up, to shout an enthusiastic "Yes" to life, just as we say "Yes" to our first cup of coffee each morning. Nothing would please Him more than for us to live fresh-brewed lives steeped with His love, filling the world with the marvelous aroma of Christ. The EZ Lesson Plan will provide humor, vignettes, and in depth study to small groups all over on this topic.

EZ Lesson Plan ISBN: 0-7852-9723-5   **Student's Guide ISBN: 0-7852-9724-3**

The Law of Respect

John C. Maxwell

AVAILABLE JULY 25, 2000

We are taught from our parents to respect others. Our business practices are to be ones of respecting others ideas, thoughts and mainly their motivations. We tend to get caught up in the daily routines, but if we do not respect those around us and the ones we work with, our success will be held at a low ebb. John Maxwell is a leader's leader.

EZ Lesson Plan ISBN: 0-7852-9756-1   **Student's Guide ISBN: 0-7852-9757-X**

Becoming A Woman of Grace

Cynthia Heald

AVAILABLE SEPTEMBER 1, 2000

This is a newly formatted product built around a message that only Cynthia Heald could deliver to us. Women have proven to be the stronger of the sexes in prayer, empathy and faith. Cynthia leads this women's group study on how a woman can become A Woman of Grace through prayer, obedience to God and other practices of their lives. This EZ Lesson Plan will bring the components of this publishing product to one, self-contained format ready to start small groups.

EZ Lesson Plan ISBN: 0-7852-9706-5   **Student's Guide ISBN: 0-7852-9707-3**

Andy Griffith Volume 2 Bible Study Series

AVAILABLE SEPTEMBER 12, 2000

Systems Media

In the Andy Griffith Volume 2 Bible Study Series you will see four great studies: First lesson: "A Wife for Andy" teaches us about integrity in looking for a spouse, as well as in handling friends a bit over-eager to see their plans to help us succeed—even if it kills us! Second lesson: "High Noon in Mayberry" illustrates the futility of worry, both in mind and in action. When Andy decides not to assume the worst, he is able to relax and enjoy the true intent of his former enemy's visit. Not so, for the posse outside his door! Third lesson: "Barney's First Car" is a roller-coaster ride of elation, dejection, amazement, and deception as Barney's friends loyally support him through his crisis. Fourth lesson: "The Great Filling Station Robbery" demonstrates the damage we can do to others' reputations when our perceptions do not keep pace with their growth.

EZ Lesson Plan ISBN: 0-8499-8832-2   **Student's Guide ISBN: 0-8499-8833-0**